Thad Barnum's lateso
the authentically rele\ 's
to be a *real* disciple— h
me they can know wh............ ....ully held by him.

Using the power of biblical and real-life stories, Thaddeus Barnum brings the mercy of God to life in this devotional. For fifty days, he will lead you to see the Lord, His people, and even your own life with new eyes—the merciful eyes of the Lord.

Thaddeus Barnum has beautifully integrated well-known and beloved Bible stories with his own pastoral experiences to dramatize the awesome mercy of our Lord and move hearts and minds in a convicting and very meaningful way. This book will compel many of us to reexamine our responsibility to pass on God's great mercy to others and commit to do more in His name.

Experiencing mercy is life transforming. When you are weary of the journey, mercy is a balm to the soul. But mercy enters another dimension when you are merciful to others. This is the deep mercy in Barnum's new book, *Real Mercy*. The wise words of this book will renew and encourage your soul.

Real Mercy is an evangelistic tool, a nurturing tool, a discipleship manual. It challenges the beneficiaries of God's mercy to be advocates of hope to the hopeless. This book tells the mercies of God in practical and real-life experience and is a testimony script for many who have come from hopelessness to hope in Christ.

After twenty years running a ministry of mercy to the unlovely, I have seen the truth of Thad Barnum's insights into our God of mercy. He carries the implications of God's attributes to a new level here and tells powerful stories to illustrate. Highly valuable.

—ED MORGAN, president of The Bowery Mission, New York

Weaving together the strands of Scripture study, journal reflection, and poignant questions, Thad models a modern method for meditation along the way. He transports the reader into the text as he explores the senses, thoughts, and emotions of the gospel stories of mercy. A must-read calling for those seeking to be merciful.

—CHRIS SHINN, co-pastor of Faith Community Church, Charleston, West Virginia

This book is for real people—those who refuse to see the mercy of God as mere flowery speech or academic metaphor. It's for those who experience God's mercy and desire to live it out in the service of others, especially the suffering in the world.

—AL TIZON, executive minister, Serve Globally; associate professor, North Park Theological Seminary

Real Mercy offers the deepest truth: Mercy is everything to Jesus. Thaddeus Barnum takes the reader on a seamless journey from familiar biblical stories to the lives of ordinary men and women in his life who are extraordinary in the power of God's mercy.

—FRANK WILLIAMS, director and United Nations representative, World Vision International

REAL MERCY

WHERE BIBLE AND LIFE MEET

THADDEUS BARNUM

wesleyan
PUBLISHING HOUSE
wphstore.com

Copyright © 2015 by Thaddeus Barnum
Published by Wesleyan Publishing House
Indianapolis, Indiana 46250
Printed in the United States of America
ISBN: 978-0-89827-916-0
ISBN (e-book): 978-0-89827-917-7

Library of Congress Cataloging-in-Publication Data

Barnum, Thaddeus.
  Real mercy : where Bible and life meet / Thaddeus Barnum.
      pages cm
  Includes bibliographical references and index.
  ISBN 978-0-89827-916-0 (pbk. : alk. paper) 1. Mercy--Meditations. 2. Mercy--Biblical
teaching. I. Title.
  BV4647.M4B37 2015
  242'.5--dc23

                              2015009228

To Barry and Kate Oches with my love

Other books by Thaddeus Barnum include:
Never Silent
Remember Eve
Where Is God in Suffering and Tragedy?
Real Identity
Real Love

For more information about these and
other discipleship resources,
visit the call2disciple ministry website at
www.call2disciple.com.

Thad's other devotionals in this Deeper Devotion series,
Real Identity and *Real Love*, are available at
wphstore.com.

CONTENTS

Free shepherding resources are available at
www.wphresources.com/realmercy.

ACKNOWLEDGEMENTS

This is my third devotional with Wesleyan Publishing House.

In *Real Identity*, I made a simple case: The Lord wants us to find our identity in Him—not in what we do, not in how others see us. In *Real Love*, this concept was taken a step further: If we know who we are in Christ, we will do what He says and love one another as He has loved us. If we did, as we must, how would church be different? How would we impact our world?

That's the story of *Real Mercy*.

At my church in Connecticut, I preached on God's character of mercy for nearly a year. I came to realize He wants His heart of mercy to change us before we do acts of mercy. The latter without the former is philanthropy. The two together bring the kingdom of God to a world in need of Jesus Christ.

As a church, we prayed, "Lord, disciple us. Make us a people of Your mercy."

Our eyes were soon opened to Christians in our church family, local community, and across the globe who were living mercy out loud. It strengthened what we were already doing in mission. But something new happened. The Lord gave our suburban church the desire to adopt a neighborhood in the city where we, too, might learn to live mercy out loud.

We spend every Saturday morning prayer walking the streets, picking up trash, building relationships, and coming alongside the local pastors and Christians to serve them. We are learning that real love is possible among Christians who don't look the same. Walls that divided us are coming down. Bridges are going up. The city is coming to the suburbs and the suburbs are coming to the city and we are learning to live real mercy together.

And our prayer continues: "Lord, disciple us. Make us a people of Your mercy."

Craig Bubeck, director of product development at Wesleyan Publishing House, let me take risks with this devotional. Each one opens with a biblical reflection before diving into a practical story where Bible and life meet. Craig, thank you for believing in me. Thanks also to the excellent staff at WPH: Rachael Stevenson (editor), Lyn Rayn (cover and interior design), and Jeff Ray and Dane Benton (sales and marketing). I love the passion at WPH to do everything possible to make discipleship resources available to churches. It's a joy to be part of the Wesleyan family.

I am indebted to Pam and Ken Blackwell, Carol and Paul Wolff, and June and Frank Williams who were the first to lead our church family into the city. I'm thankful also for Cindy and Patrick Robbers, Success and David Smith, and Cathea and Michael Jackson—the first pastors who opened their arms to welcome us into their neighborhood. They continually show us the mercy of our Lord Jesus Christ, and we are changed by it.

Erilynne, thank you for your love. It is an honor to be your husband. And it's a joy to serve alongside you, our board, and staff at call2disciple.

Now dear reader, will you come with me? Let us dig deep into the gospel stories where the God of mercy himself has come among us. He will show us everything we need. But I will warn you now: It's risky. If you dig too deep, He will change you. He will change your church family. Then He will send you. Are you ready for that? If so, risk the prayer: "Lord, disciple me. Make me a person of Your mercy."

INTRODUCTION

Freely you received, freely give.
—MATTHEW 10:8

There is a kind of mercy we can't express in our own strength. It belongs to God. It is given by God—freely. All we have to do is receive it. And when we do, the miraculous happens: God changes us on the inside.

He makes us a people of mercy.

And suddenly the motion begins. As we receive, we give. It's how His mercy works. We can't hold on to it. We can't horde it or hide it or keep it to ourselves. When we have it and are changed by it, we give it as freely as we received it.

But there are people . . .

Jesus warned us about them. There are people who receive but never *receive*. There's no miracle. There's no change. This, Jesus explained in great detail, is the story of a wicked slave. We are not to be like him (see part 2).

But our Lord didn't leave us with that warning. He also told the story of a son, a lost son, who found his way home again. This young man knew, deep in his soul, he didn't deserve his family's compassion and mercy. But it came, in full; and willingly, joyfully, he opened his arms and received it (see part 3).

This is everything.

It's the very heart and soul of the good news: "But God, being rich in mercy, because of the great love with which he loved us, even when we were dead in our trespasses, made us alive together with Christ" (Eph. 2:4–5 ESV).

And when it comes to us, we are made new.

That change is visible. It reshapes how we think, how we act, how we engage the world around us, and all of these things to our very core. This mercy shapes our character. We see it in the royal line of Jesus' own family (see part 4). We find it in people we least expect—those we've labeled and pushed away (see part 5).

It's meant to be in us.

And the only way for that to happen is to let mercy come. He—the person of mercy himself—must do with us what He came to do (see part 6). And when He does, one taste of it in our souls, and Micah 6:8 comes alive. He gives us everything we need to act justly, love mercy, and walk humbly with our God.

And out we go—a people of mercy to live mercy. We are men and women on Matthew 10:8 mission (see part 7), holding in our hearts God's eternal promise: "His mercies never come to an end; they are new every morning" (Lam. 3:22–23 ESV).

New and full of surprise.

For this is our God! And He zealously wants us to hear with His ears and see with His eyes. Just as He did in the simple story of a blind beggar (see part 1).

A person no one sees.

With a cry no one hears: "Jesus, Son of David, have mercy on me!"

But Jesus is like no one else. He sees. He hears. Mercy is everything to Him. He wants it to be everything to us. So we must start here, outside the town of Jericho, with a man on the side of the road, begging.

And let the story of real mercy change us forever.

PART 1

A BLIND
BEGGAR

1

TO LOVE MERCY: A STORY

*And what does the L*ORD *require of you? To act justly and*
to love mercy and to walk humbly with your God.

—MICAH 6:8 NIV

I didn't understand it at first. Isn't mercy something
we do?

I see mercy in my Aunt Barbie and Uncle Paul. Their
love for the Lord led them to start two mission centers in
Colorado that serve hot meals and provide food, clothing,
toys, blankets, counseling, and financial assistance to those
in need.

It's what my sister Kate does every day in her social work.
Her big heart of love overflows with compassion for the rural
elderly in southern Ohio. It's seen in my dad every Wednesday
night as he serves the poor in Stamford, Connecticut.

This I get. It's what Christians do: We remember the
needs of the poor (Gal. 2:10).

I was thirty-four, pastoring a church in Pittsburgh, when
the "lightbulb" went on. I happened to be listening to a visiting
preacher from East Africa. He urgently tasked all church

leaders to build "the character of God's mercy in the Christian soul." He went on to say, "If we're going to tell people about Jesus, they need to see Jesus in us. If we've recieved His mercy, we must be a people of mercy." I liked it—a lot. I wrote it in my journal. I thought I knew what the preacher meant. But truth be told, I didn't. Not until I saw it the eyes of one man.

Jared.

We met coincidentally. In March 1991, my friend Bob was in the hospital dying of lung cancer. He'd been diagnosed just after Christmas. On his last Sunday in church, he got on his knees next to his wife, Dot, and prayed as Jesus prayed, "Heavenly Father, not my will be done, but Thine."[1]

And now, in March in the hospital, he was in a coma. The doctors said it wouldn't be long.

In the bed next to Bob sat a twenty-eight-year-old man named Jared. The young man sat hunched over, his face down, his legs outstretched, fighting for breath. His cancer had already taken his left arm and collapsed one lung. It was easier for him to breathe bent over. Easier not to talk.

But he was beautiful. His eyes were huge, set to perfection above high cheek bones and a strong, chiseled face with cocoa brown skin stretched tightly over each bone. There was gentleness in his face—even as he struggled for breath.

That afternoon, I heard Jared's phone ring.

"May I answer it for you?" I asked. He nodded, and I soon told him, "Your wife wants you to know she loves you. She'll be in about quarter to seven." He reached for my hand, squeezed it, and whispered, "That was nice of you."

I blurted out, almost selfishly, "How do you do it, Jared?"

He lifted his head, looked me in the eyes, and said, "Jesus is all I've got."

I already knew this about him. His family was a Christian family. His mother told me Jared had given his life to Jesus as a young man. "He did everything right," she said, and then she talked about his time in the military; his marriage to a lovely woman, a nurse; and their two children, both under the age of five.

"He wanted to see his children grow," she said, "and that's not going to happen. He knows that now. We all do."

Even so, I didn't understand it. It scared me to think of myself suffering as Jared was suffering. Would I be able to say what he just said to me?

As the day went on, in that same room, my friend Bob and his family faced deepening trials of their own.

By 3:00 in the morning, while he was still deep in a coma, Bob's breathing started to slow. Dot was the only one with him. She sat at his bedside, holding her husband's hand, her chair next to the curtain that separated him from Jared. She leaned her head on the bed and began to cry.

Then came a familiar sound—the curtain rings sliding on metal. And then she felt it. A hand—Jared's only hand—gently resting on her shoulder. Softly patting, tenderly rubbing, as a son would comfort his mother. She could feel his warmth. She reached up, covered his hand with hers, and turned to look at him. There was enough light to see his beautiful eyes.

"He's all we've got," Jared quietly whispered.

It was like medicine from heaven to her soul.

By morning's light, Bob had somehow come out of his coma, and he would spend the next six weeks at home before he passed into the arms of the Lord.

For Jared, however, the story was different.

On the very next night, the curtain stayed closed between us. His family never left his side. When morning came again, the curtain was finally pushed back, just long enough for the briefest glimpse. It was the first time we'd seen Jared lying down—peacefully. No more struggles. No more gasps of air. No more sleepless nights to come. The watch was over.

But I have never forgotten him. Or that hand stretched out in the night.

He's the one who showed me that mercy isn't first what we do. It's who we are. It's who the God of mercy makes us in Christ. Because of Jared, I began praying the prayer the East African preacher taught me to pray: "Build the character of Your mercy in me—and in us, Your people."

For this is where it all begins.

QUESTIONS FOR REFLECTION*

Mercy is a common word, known and experienced by all people. But the mercy God gives is different. What changes in your life if you let God make you a person of mercy?

How did Jared do this—show mercy even in his suffering? What are you like when you suffer? Why do we long for mercy more than give mercy?

NOTE

1. Thaddeus Barnum, *Where Is God in Suffering and Tragedy?* (DeBary, FL: Longwood Communications, 1997), 254–257, 266–269.

---

* *The reflection questions at the end of each devotion are designed to encourage prayer, journaling, and conversation in small group settings. It's easy to read and go on. It's better to read, stop, and engage in dialogue and prayer.*

2

AT THE OFFICE

Reflections on Luke 18:35

A blind man was sitting by the road begging.

—LUKE 18:35

If only I could interview the blind man:

"I was wondering, sir, how you got here this morning. Did friends bring you? Same ones each day? Or do you have to beg for that, too? And where did you spend the night? Do you have a home? Do you sleep in a bed with a roof over your head, a fire in the fireplace? Did you wake to a warm meal? Are you hungry, even now? Do you have any family or friends who love you? Care for you?

"Or are you, as I fear, homeless?

"Has it always been this way? Were you born blind, or did it happen later in life? Perhaps an accident of some kind? Maybe you had a good childhood? Or, did you have to start begging even then? Have people been kind to you, or do they make you feel like an outcast? Maybe less than human? As if God has forsaken you?"

I wonder how old he was when he met Jesus. I wonder why Luke, the gospel writer, didn't give him a name.

Mark said he had a cloak (see Mark 10:50). I wonder if it was his only possession. Was it his roof in the rain; his warmth in the cold; his knapsack to carry a beggar's haul at day's end; his one secret hiding place—dug deep under its cover—where he could dream of a world where he was known, honored, and loved? A respectable man! A Jewish man whose prayers at synagogue actually reached the throne of almighty God. I see him there, just outside Jericho, begging. Perhaps I could say his office door was open for business.

He begged like half the modern world today begs. By all reports, half and more of the planet's population in the twenty-first century lives below the poverty line in need of food, clean water, vaccines, basic health care, a sustainable job, and a kind remembrance that they too were made in God's perfect image. He, like all of them, waited for someone to pass by and show mercy.

He irritated me.

I was attending a pastors' conference. It was my job to introduce him as the keynote speaker that morning and open the session in prayer. Since I knew nothing about him, he provided a sheet of paper that listed his accomplishments. They were most impressive.

He was everything I am not. Tall, handsome, with an athletic build and lovely smile—like he'd just come off a photo shoot for a magazine cover. He had a beautiful tenor voice, soothing and strong. As he began speaking, he oozed charisma. He was funny, engaging, self-deprecating, and, at times, deeply moved by emotion. The crowd laughed, cried, and, at the end, rose in a standing ovation.

Afterward, I overheard a pastor say, "That was the best ever! If I had half his talent, our church would be filled every Sunday." Another said, "I could listen to him all day long. He was eloquent, entrancing, hysterical, and completely delightful!" A young pastor agreed: "He's exactly what my generation needs." I was horrified. This preacher did what no preacher should ever do. He left us talking about *him*.

I vented with a friend—also a pastor—over lunch.

"I think you're jealous," he said, poking. "The man's a consummate performer. He's got a huge church in the Midwest. People adore him everywhere he goes. Now, what could be better than that? I bet most preachers dream of being like him."

I was too agitated to poke back.

"There was a preacher from my grandfather's generation," I told him, "who pulled me aside one day and gave me sound advice. 'Your job is to preach the gospel. Point to Him—not yourself. Remember what the apostle Paul said in 2 Corinthians 4:5: "For we do not preach ourselves but Christ Jesus as Lord." But,' he warned, 'it won't be easy. Pride will dog you your entire life. It's subtle. It's strong. It's a deep pull inside all of us. We want the attention, the applause, the approval.'"

My friend admitted candidly, "He's exactly right. I fight it all the time."

"But you saw what happened today," I replied. "This man's job was to open the Scriptures to us. He didn't do it. He told stories for an hour. And worse, a congregation full of pastors didn't even notice. They didn't care. They loved it."

"Absolutely!" He smiled in jest. "He made us feel good about ourselves."

I sat back, wishing he'd take my concern more seriously.

"So, you don't wrestle with this?" he began with a touch of challenge. "There isn't a little tiny piece of you longing for recognition and praise? I don't believe it."

"You're changing the subject," I protested.

"Am I? Are you sure you're not the least bit jealous?"

I did my best to ignore him. But as far back as I can remember I've always been confused by this. I'm part of a denomination that teaches that pastors are servants. We serve the people. We never exalt ourselves. We do as our Lord did and lead by serving.

But the one who is the greatest among you must become like the youngest, and the leader like the servant. For who is greater, the one who reclines at the table or the one who serves? Is it not the one who reclines at the table? But I am among you as the one who serves.

—LUKE 22:26–27

But it's odd. We say one thing and do another.

For example, my denomination has the most elaborate ordination services. First to deacon, then presbyter. For some, bishop and, for a small few, archbishop. We dress in fine robes. We distinguish ourselves from those not ordained.

Then we stand in lofty pulpits and tell people we're here to serve.

It confuses me. Always has. Aren't we actually lifting ourselves up? Older pastors wisely taught me. "We don't step up the ladder of success," they'd say. "We step down, just as our Lord did."

For you know the grace of our Lord Jesus Christ, that though He was rich, yet for your sake He became poor.

—2 CORINTHIANS 8:9

"But then how do you handle all the attention?" I asked them, knowing many of them experienced great success in ministry, pastoring large congregations.

"By keeping focus," they'd advise me. "Simply remember how the apostle Paul answered your question."

So we speak, not as pleasing men, but God who examines our hearts. For we never came with flattering speech, as you know, nor with a pretext for greed— God is witness—nor did we seek glory from men.

—1 THESSALONIANS 2:4–6

"If you're out to please men—entertain them!" they went on. "Tell them a joke! Get them to love you. But if you want to please God, if you want His approval more than theirs, then do what He has called you to do. Be real. Be faithful. Give them the saving message of Jesus Christ. Point them to Him so when you're done, they're only talking about Him."

So I did my best, as a young minister in my twenties.

But looking back over the years, I see now what I didn't want to see then. My motives were not always pure. As much as I felt called to follow their example and heed their counsel, I secretly wanted what they had. It was there, a small flame burning inside me, a quiet longing to have a big congregation just like them. Yes, me too—a beggar on the side of the road—begging for attention. Begging for approval.

I was young, and I guess you could say I opened my office door for business. I sincerely believed in my heart the cheering was only and all for Jesus Christ. But in truth, I wanted the tiniest little bit for me.

QUESTIONS FOR REFLECTION

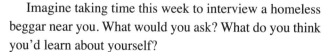

Imagine taking time this week to interview a homeless beggar near you. What would you ask? What do you think you'd learn about yourself?

What happens if you let someone interview you? Where are the places of longing and begging inside your heart?

3

DISTANT THUNDER

Reflections on Luke 18:36–37

Now hearing a crowd going by,
he began to inquire what this was.

—LUKE 18:36

I'm guessing he heard it before anyone else could see it. In the distance, he picked up a sound that was different—but what? Like a storm way out on the horizon whispering its terrors that something was there. Perhaps he strained to hear above the conversations and movements around him. It had all the feel of a swarm of people, their collective voices making a sound he couldn't distinguish. Were they coming here? How many and why? Would they see him and respect his space?

The sound like thunder grew louder.

"What's coming?" he inquired, wanting someone to see for him.

Soon enough, there was another sound. Then the ground underneath told more of the story. He could feel the vibration of people running toward him. Perhaps he heard voices more clearly too, high pitched with excitement. A crowd was forming. Whatever was out there in the distance, the people around him now saw it. A crowd was gathering to join the crowd coming.[1]

"Somebody tell me what's going on!" he shouted, wanting someone to hear him, but still no one answered.

The sounds close by drowned out the sounds in the distance. His space continued to fill with people. Perhaps he felt them brushing by. I wonder if he was scared. Masses of people on the move can endanger the blind. All because they're looking elsewhere. They wouldn't see him sitting on the ground. They wouldn't look down. They'd push. They'd fight for the front. They wouldn't realize that in their frenzy to see they were trampling down those who couldn't see.

Perhaps he shouted all the more. Not for mercy. Not for alms. Just to survive. "If they hear me," perhaps he thought, "maybe they'll see me and not hurt me." It was coming closer now. I imagine him reaching out and grabbing someone tight when they jostled him, saying, "What's happening here?" And finally a voice comes back with surprising kindness.

Jesus of Nazareth is passing by.

I sent a note to my pastor friend.

Eric,

Your question has haunted me these past few days. Do I wrestle for recognition and praise? Yes, I guess so.

I've been spending time recently in Luke's story of the blind man. As I pictured the large crowds around him, I couldn't help hearing the sounds of people cheering for Jesus. As I did, I was suddenly struck by your question and wondered if I needed a sliver of those cheers for myself.

I see it when I look back on my life—clear as day. I always wanted the popularity of the preachers who mentored me. But if you had asked me then, I'd have denied it—absolutely. Am I denying it now?

Talk to me?
Thad

A few days later, he responded.

Thad,

I told you I fight this all the time. There are a host of reasons why. The first is the most obvious: We are sinful people. Our hearts are empty. We need the One who made us to fill us, and nothing else satisfies. But we tend to do what we always do and push Him away, filling our hearts with other things.

Things that never satisfy. We need Him. I need Him.

My story is simple. I crave attention. Always have. But for me it's more than the size of the crowd or the sound of their cheers. I want to know who's in the crowd. I want somebody of reputation, someone well-known and respected, to like me. That's my issue. I want somebody who is somebody to think I'm some-body too.

So if I were in Luke's story, I'd be studying the crowd. I'd be looking for the well-dressed dignitaries. I'll take their cheers. You can have the rest. Deal?

Eric

Like always, Eric surprised me, digging deeper than I wanted to go. I read it again and thought, "Who does this? Who openly confesses, 'I crave attention'?"

I wonder if that's me too. I don't think I've ever talked to anybody about this subject before, but even if I did, I'd probably say what Eric just said. Jesus is the only One who satisfies our deepest need for approval. No one else can. I knew that. Eric knew that. So why does he press so hard?

Odd to remember it now, but Pastor George came to mind. Eric and I attended his retirement party. He'd served fifty years as a clergyman. All George could talk about that night was George—endlessly. We sat there listening to all the places he'd been and all the people he'd met—world leaders, presidents, senators, newsmakers—and he made it sound like they were his closest friends.

"Don't let me get like that!" I whispered to Eric as George droned on.

"A clear case of M.A.D.," Eric whispered back.

"What's that?"

He rolled his eyes, grimaced, and said, "Massive approval disorder!"

I laughed—as quietly as I could.

"Yeah, probably shouldn't have said that!" Eric admitted to me when I got him on the phone the next day and reminded him of his diagnosis of Pastor George. "Especially since I have the same disorder."

"Not like him," I said, reassuringly.

"A lot like him," he responded. "Maybe the only difference is I know I have it."

When he heard my silence on the other end of the phone, he continued. "You remember my story, right? My aunt and uncle raised me. I call them 'Mom' and 'Dad,' but they're not really. My parents didn't want me. They split up after I was born. My aunt and uncle took me in and raised me with my cousins, who were pretty close to me in age. I actually have never met my parents."

"Yeah, I remember."

"Ever since, I've fought this craving for attention, needing to be needed, wanting people that matter to see me, recognize me, like me. It's why I first went into ministry. I met a lot of pastors like George—adored by crowds, recognized by the elite of society. I wanted that in my life; same thing."

"That's why you went into ministry?"

"I came to Christ three years *after* I was ordained!"

"That's right; I forgot."

"Yeah, all because of this. The Lord finally showed me the abandonment I felt as a child, that sense of being tossed away by my parents, was profoundly controlling my life and hurting people I love. So, when I needed someone's approval, I'd stomp over anybody just to get it, and I really didn't care."

"So what did you do?"

"I called a friend." And with that, he painted a picture that, once again, quietly stabbed at my own heart. I put his words in my journal late that same night:

"If we could climb back into Luke's story of the blind man," Eric said, "then you'd see the change that was

starting in me. *My friend helped me stop pretending I was a disciple of Jesus when I really wasn't. He helped me stop needing the cheers of others when really what I needed was Jesus Christ himself.*

"So picture me as one of the faces in the crowd. See me as one of the lucky ones who pushed, shoved, and fought my way to the front so Jesus could see me when He passed by. That's my story. And it's not a perfect story. I'm the same guy who stepped on the blind man just to get to Jesus. I was all about me—only me.

"I was, to use your analogy, the distant storm, the distant thunder, that came and rolled right over him."

QUESTIONS FOR REFLECTION

Consider the implied danger of the crowds surrounding the blind man. Share a time when your needs blinded you to others around you who were in need.

When has the need for approval controlled you? When have you received approval at the expense of someone else?

NOTE

1. Both Matthew 20:29 and Mark 10:46 give us the picture of a large crowd around Jesus and His disciples. In the same way, Luke 18:39 and Mark 10:48 show a crowd around the beggar awaiting Jesus' coming.

4

SLAPPED DOWN

Reflections on Luke 18:38–39

And he cried out, "Jesus, Son of David, have mercy on me!"
And those who were in front rebuked him, telling him to be silent.

—LUKE 18:38–39 ESV

I see him there, clutching his cloak, hunkering down in survival mode, praying to God for the crowds to pass and leave him alone.

But at the sound of Jesus' name, all that changed. It was Jesus. He was there, almost right in front of him, maybe less than a stone's throw away. And in between was a thick wall of people towering over him. Jesus would not see him. Nor would He hear him; how could He? Surely everyone was getting louder the closer He came. But still the man knew, He's here! Jesus is here!

Perhaps he tossed the cloak down in front of him and got up on his knees. His hands stretched toward the sky. His head lifted up and his mouth wide open as he blended his voice into a sea of voices crying out for the Nazarene to stop.

"Jesus, Son of David, have mercy on me!" he cried out over and over again. But the more he did, the louder he got, the more he irritated the people in front of him. As some point, they turned back and rebuked him.

Was it done in anger? Were their words harsh? How many were they? Did the force of their words—strong and insistent—

*push him back, slap him down, and make him feel worthless?
Voiceless?*

*These voices, he knew, continue. They were his people, from
his town, the same ones who passed by every day and showed
him mercy. Mercy with a coin or two. Mercy with a word of kindness and pity. These were the ones who kept him alive. He
needed them. So why wouldn't they show him mercy now? Why
wouldn't they lead him to the front and let him be seen by the
One who could make him see?*

Slapped down.

*But mercy was on their terms, not his. And he'd get their
mercy tomorrow if he did what they told him to do today. For this
was mercy not from his equals but from his masters—and they
gave him no choice. He had to please them. It was business. It
was politics. It was survival. Play the game and win. Resist and
suffer the consequences. It was a beggar's life. It's how mercy
works in his world.*

*Always slapped down. Left in the dust, hidden from sight.
As Jesus passed by.*

"These are mostly Eric's issues, not mine," I told
myself, but I knew differently. It didn't take me long to
prove the point. Frustrated with myself, I wrote Eric.

Eric,

*Had coffee at a diner with Dana yesterday. Did you
hear he lost his job again? Third one in eighteen months.
He's taking it hard. Poor guy has zero self-esteem. His
ex-wife's breathing down his neck for money. She tells*

him he's a failure at everything he does—husband, father, provider—and he feels every bit of it.

All I know is he knows Jesus. All I want to do is encourage him. It's why we're having coffee.

But what happens? Bobby Taylor comes over to our table. Great guy, impressive guy, pastor of the Baptist church in town. He just got back from India, where the Lord powerfully used his team to bring tons of people to Christ. He beamed with excitement as he told a few stories from his trip. I asked if he could stay.

"I've got to go," he said. "But tell me how you're doing."

I couldn't help myself. I tried to impress him by telling my own stories of what the Lord is doing at our church. As I talked, his face lit up. He slapped my hand with a high five, wished us both well, and was gone. It made me feel really good.

I turned back and saw Dana hunched over the table and staring blankly into his empty coffee cup. "You OK?" I asked stupidly.

"What do you think?" he blurted.

"I don't know," I said quickly.

He then fired a piercing gaze right through me, and I knew I'd hurt him. "Too bad you're here with me," he said, his eyes still fixed on mine. "I'm not exactly one of the shining stories at our church. If I was, you could have impressed him more."

"That's not true!" I reacted.

But he was right. I did everything I could to impress Bobby Taylor. I wanted that high five, and I got it. But why—why did I do that? And why do it in front of Dana? How could I have forgotten him and his suffering? He already feels like a failure. And here I am, adding to his grief.

In my view, I did exactly what the crowd did to the blind beggar. I pushed him back so I could push myself forward. It makes me wonder, who's really blind in Luke's story? I'm thinking it's the crowd in front of the beggar. Today, it feels like me.

Thad

Eric e-mailed me and asked, "Mind if I share your note with Missy?"

"Not at all," I responded, and to my surprise, Eric's wife, Missy, wrote next.

Dear Thad,

Thanks for letting me read what you wrote Eric.

I can't believe you froze the frame on the blind man when he was rebuked by the crowd in front of him. Did you know most of us never recover from that?

We get pushed down and that's our place. We spend the rest of our lives there. We do what the people in charge of us tell us to do. If we please them, it goes well for us. If we fight back, we may gain some ground. But not much.

Eventually, we learn it's easier to stay put and be quiet.

Every once in a while, people come along who fight the system. They stand up and push back those who push them down. I have a dear friend like that. All her life, she's been ruled by strong men. Her father's voice is the loudest. He loves her, but he believes women have their place in society and in church.

She disagrees. She fights him on it, and he fights back with the deadliest weapon of all. He stops loving her. So she pushes harder. She slowly rose to leadership in her church and eventually got ordained. Her father stopped speaking to her.

Sadly, he died before they could resolve it.

"I want you to be part of this movement," my friend told me over lunch.

Part of me wants to. I actually agree with much of what she says. But not like this. I'm not a fighter. I'm not convinced the Lord wants us to fight those who slap us down and push us back. If we do, they define us. They steal our hearts. I won't let them have that kind of power over me. At the same time, I don't believe I'm supposed to just sit there in the dust and do nothing. There's a better way. I believe the beggar of Luke 18 chose that better way.

So I do what he did: Jesus is passing by, and I choose Him.

"But I am part of this movement," I insisted, as I held up a glass of cold ice tea. "I'm your friend!" I told her.

She smiled, clinked her glass to mine, and said, "Yes, you are!"

Sometimes I wonder if she'll ever recover. The wounds inflicted by her father are deep and decades old. But I stay close to her. I'm on a mission. I have a cause, and for this, I guess you might say I am every bit a fighter.

I point her to Jesus. I tell her He's passing by.

And then I pray that maybe today, maybe for a second or two, she'll take her eyes off her oppressors and put them on the One who can heal her tired soul.

Missy

QUESTIONS FOR REFLECTION

Why do you think the crowd rebuked the blind man? Why deny him access to Jesus? When was the last time you slapped down someone?

Do you have oppressors in your life? Have you ever felt trapped by them with no way out? What does it take to get your eyes off them and onto Jesus?

5

DEEP WITHIN

~~~

Reflections on Luke 18:39

Yet he screamed and shrieked so much the more,
Son of David, take pity and have mercy on me!

—LUKE 18:39 AMP

Did anyone speak to him as he lay there in the dust?

Maybe a kind, reasonable voice: "Stay down. It'll all be over soon. Tomorrow your friends will still be your friends. They'll care for you—you'll still have food." Or maybe the exact opposite: "Who are they to slap you down like that? Do something! You are just as much a son of Abraham as they are. Fight them!"

If so, he listened to neither.

Instead, he seemed to shoot back into the air like a kite launching into the sky. I see him there, on his knees again, his hands outstretched, his face surprisingly happy and free as he opened his mouth and let out a scream, a shriek: "Son of David, take pity and have mercy on me!"

This time, I hear what I didn't hear before—I wonder why? He calls Jesus "Son of David." I read through the Gospels of Matthew, Mark, Luke, and John. I discover that few people knew this secret about Jesus. Of course, the angel Gabriel did, as he announced Jesus' birth to Mary. So did the children and the crowd on Palm Sunday. There were a few others, but not many. Why?

Why did few see as the blind beggar saw?

His voice, like a musical note lifting high above the roar of the crowd, pierced the air with a sound no one else even knew how to play: he was calling on the Son of David! He was telling everybody, "This is our King! This is He whom David and all the prophets foretold would come. He has mercy to give like no other mercy."

How did the blind man know this? Who told him? And when?

I wonder if the crowd in front did it again. Did they push him back, push him down, slam him hard to the ground? Did they threaten him this time? Did they hurt him? No matter, he didn't stop. No one could steal the gift he'd been given.

"Son of David, take pity and have mercy on me!"

Deep within, he knew what few knew. He saw what few saw.

A day passes, and then another. I want to write Missy back, but I don't know what to say yet. I keep thinking about her friend.

Is it true some of us never recover?

I also keep thinking about the beggar. How did he break free from this tension, both refusing to stay down and refusing to fight the crowd in front of him? He didn't seem to care about them. In fact, he ignored them. He went a different path, opting for a third choice I didn't even know was available.

He was free. He was loud. I want that in my life.

So I called up Eric and set a date for dinner with our wives. It was a good choice. We had a good night together.

The next morning, I tried to capture part of our conversation in my journal. There were things said I didn't want to forget. Here is what I recorded:

Halfway through dinner, I asked Missy about her friend.

Missy: "She's doing well, I think. I saw her the other day. She gave a Bible teaching at her church. She's a phenomenal teacher. People respond well to her. For me, I'm a little too sensitive. I hear the edge in her voice."

Erilynne: "What kind of edge?"

Missy: "Like she's arguing with somebody who's not there.

Eric: "Do you think she's aware of it?"

Missy: "Maybe a little. I've talked to her about it. 'That edge,' she tells me, 'gives women hope!' Then she tells me, 'Too many women are suffering from abuse like I did. They need to know the Lord is for them, not against them.' And she's right. But I know that militant tone in her voice. I've experienced it. It's coming from a wounding in her soul that I know the Lord wants to heal."

Erilynne: "It sounds exhausting."

Missy: "For me, it was. But my story pales in comparison to hers. Although my dad was an alcoholic, I knew he loved me. I knew he always loved me. Growing up, there were times he was sober and times he wasn't. And when he wasn't, it was bad. He never hurt me. I just remember being scared."

Eric: "He had a lot of good years at the end of his life."

Missy: "But a few months before he died, he relapsed. It got so bad he ended up in the hospital and shut all of us out. I'm guessing he was ashamed. My mom, sisters, and I figured he'd come around eventually. We gave him his space. Next thing we know, we were told he'd had a heart attack and died. I can't even begin to describe the shock.

"A few weeks after the funeral, we were cleaning out his things and I found a notebook in his desk drawer. I could tell by his penmanship he was drunk when he wrote most of it. But there were things in it about me— hateful things. I tried to tell myself he wasn't in his right mind. But the rejection really hurt. It sent me into years of battling anger."

Eric: "Really hard years. You might say she had an 'edge.'"

Erilynne: "Like your friend."

Missy: "Yeah, a little. For me, I'd explode at Eric or the kids over stupid things. It was always there, just under the surface. It became part of me. I held on to it, like I needed it. For years Eric tried to help me. He'd tell me the kids were growing up scared of setting me off. I tried to change but couldn't. It got so bad I had to finally get on my knees in church one day and beg Jesus for help. I don't know exactly how it happened, but it did. I saw what I couldn't see before. My eyes were suddenly fixed on my heavenly Dad, not my earthly dad. I realized He hadn't rejected me. I don't know how I knew it.

But I felt like all I had to do was ask Him for His blessing and He'd give it."

Eric: "And you've been free ever since."

Missy: "It changed everything. It even changed how
I saw my father. I knew he loved me. I knew what he
wrote when he was drunk wasn't true. But even if it
was, his rejection no longer controlled me. The Lord
had my heart and all I can say is I was healed. And
that's what I want for my friend.

"I want her to know the King is passing. He has
mercy to give. And He can do, deep in the soul, what
none of us can do."

QUESTIONS FOR REFLECTION

What a miracle! The blind man sees Jesus as the promised
King. What is your story? When did your eyes of faith open
to see Jesus?

It takes real choice to get our eyes off those who hurt
us and fix them on our heavenly Father. What practical
things can help you make that choice today?

6

WHEN KINDNESS STOPPED

Reflections on Mark 10:49

And Jesus stopped and said, "Call him here."
So they called the blind man, saying to him,
"Take courage, stand up! He is calling for you."

—MARK 10:49

It was almost over.

The crowd coming, the crowd here, then blending into one and moving together. Jesus was passing now. People were everywhere—absolutely everywhere—straining to see Him, pressing and pushing as crowds do. Would He see their sick? Would He stop and heal them? Would something happen if they touched His robe? If He did it elsewhere, would He do it here? This was it. One chance. Before He passed.

Lost in the dust of the back row, the beggar continued to cry out. The crowd washed over him like a giant ocean wave—pounding, trampling, hurting. It was almost over.

I wonder what it was like to see Jesus. Did He stand out? Was it obvious which one was Him? What was He doing—was He talking to His disciples? Was He engaging the crowd? Was He moved by those who'd fought their way to the front?

And the sound—when did He hear the sound?

Did it first register on His face? And how did He hear it? Was it with His physical ears—but how could He? The crowd was too big, too loud. Or did He hear by the still small voice of the Holy Spirit? However it happened, He heard. He stopped. Did the crowd stop with Him? Did their collective voice quiet a little?

Again, I wonder, did He lift His hand to hush the crowd even more? Did He want everyone to hear what He heard? That sound, that magnificent sound, as clear as a note of a trumpet rising over the people, announcing the King's presence.

"Jesus, Son of David . . ."

Somebody here knew Him. Perhaps He looked in the direction of the sound. But who in front could see the trumpeter buried in the back?

"Have mercy. Take pity. Be kind to me."

With that, the King issued a command: "Call him here." And those standing near the beggar, the same ones who had pushed him down, now raised him up. Their voices, which moments before had rebuked him, now thrilled with excitement: "Take courage, blind man! Cheer up! Stand on your feet. He is calling for you."

And the trumpeter stopped his playing.

He felt the hands that had slapped him down now clapped tight in his, strong and firm, bringing him up, dusting him off, patting him on the back, and guiding him hurriedly into the audience of the King. They were helping not hurting. How was that possible? And they were telling him news—unimaginable news.

Kindness had come and stopped for him.

Not long after our meal together, I wrote Eric a brief note:

Eric,

The beggar's story troubles me. Here's why.

I think many of us are like Missy's friend. We spend the best years of our lives trying to get the right people in the right places to like us. We work hard on how we look, where we live, what we do, who we know, and how much we have. Most of us don't even know we're doing it. A man once said to me, "People are going to be impressed with my obituary!" Stupid me, I laughed. I thought he was joking.

He wasn't.

Truth be told, I'm not sure I'm all that different. I think I've spent most of my life trying to impress others and not seeing the blind beggars all around me. I fear I've trampled them down without even knowing it.

Thad

The next day, Eric wrote me back:

Thad,

I wonder if I ever told you the story of my friend Zan.

He worked part time at our church—cleaning, doing odd jobs. I saw him on occasion, waved, maybe said hi, but nothing more. I was an assistant pastor in those days, and the church was so big, so busy, I barely noticed him.

Over time, I learned he was divorced, living on his own, maybe in his early sixties.

Then one day, I heard he was in the hospital—heart attack. I remember praying for him, but that's about it. I never went to visit him. A month later, he was back at work. Somebody told me he was doing much better.

"He's a smoker," they smirked. "Probably what caused it."

I didn't think much of it. But weeks later, I was sitting on the steps outside the church feeling like the weight of the world had come crashing down on me. I'd just learned a twenty-year-old college student named Whit had died in a car accident. She was an incredibly gifted young lady with a family who adored her. I was so lost in grief I had no idea he was standing there.

"I heard about Whit," he said awkwardly when I looked up. "I'm sorry."

"Thanks," I said and, trying to make conversation, I asked, "Are you OK? I heard you were in the hospital."

"I am. It was scary, but the Lord was kind to me."

I looked at him, I mean, really looked at him. All these years, he's been a nobody hardly anybody ever sees. And somehow, his words caught me. "How has He been kind to you?" I blurted, almost rudely.

And then he shared his story. All of it. Growing up poor, an alcoholic father, a working mother, a high school dropout who went into the military, married the most beautiful girl in the entire world, had two healthy and great kids—"well, mostly great"—only to have his wife leave him for another man.

"I started drinking like my father. For years I couldn't think straight. But a day came when I finally did what my grandmother taught me to do. I got on my knees and asked Jesus to have mercy on me."

And then he smiled a sheepish smile, put his head down, and blushed like somebody who didn't deserve what he'd been given.

I wanted to blush back.

What kind of person am I? Why have I pushed this man away? Why have I been blind to the one the Lord sees and unkind to the one the Lord has been kind to? All I can say is he has been my friend ever since. And he has taught me to pray: "Lord, help me see."

Eric

QUESTIONS FOR REFLECTION

Jesus sees those we can't see. Do we want to see? What can we do about our blindness—especially to the marginalized, forgotten, and needy?

It takes courage to face our blindness. When have you asked what Eric did: "Lord, why have I been unkind to the ones You have been kind to?"

7
I WANT TO SEE

Reflections on Mark 10:50 and Luke 18:40–42

Throwing aside his cloak, he jumped up and came to Jesus. . . .
And when he came near, He questioned him, "What do you
want Me to do for you?" And he said, "Lord, I want to
regain my sight!" And Jesus said to him, "Receive
your sight; your faith has made you well."

—MARK 10:50; LUKE 18:40–42

Every eye was fixed on the beggar.

The crowd between Jesus and the blind man must have parted like the Red Sea. At once everybody turned to see this man moving toward Jesus—perhaps like a child exploding into joy.

"Son of David . . ."

We can see him now, looking every bit the beggar—clothes, hair, dirt, bare feet. But what about his face? Was it wild and shocked? Was there a smile stretching ear to ear in a blaze of happiness? Was it possible he was almost singing the refrain over and over, "He's calling for me!"

Only seconds passed before the two men stood face-to-face. Perhaps people grew quieter, waiting to see what Jesus would do. I wonder, did the blind man fall to his knees? Isn't that what we do in the presence of a King? And did he lift his hands into the air—as is the custom of beggars?

"Son of David, Lord, please . . ."

And I wonder what went through our Lord's mind when He first saw him. He'd once asked His disciples, "Do you know who

I am?" And Peter knew. And Jesus told him how he knew: "My Father told you that. He whispered in your ear and let you see what only few see and know what only few know" (see Matt. 16:15–17). Just like this blind man. Jesus saw he had faith to see what nobody else in the crowd could see.

Of course, He didn't need to use words. He could have touched his eyes and been done with it. But instead He examined him. I imagine it like a script from a play:

THE KING: *What do you want Me to do for you?*
THE MAN: *I want to see.*
THE KING: *You already see. Everybody here thinks they see—but they can't—you can. They're the blind ones. Not you.*
THE MAN: *Have mercy, my Lord.*
THE KING: *Mercy has already come. My Father has opened the eyes of your heart and given you faith to see all you need to see.*
THE MAN: *But, my Lord, please. I want to see.*
THE KING: *(And with that, the King, moved with compassion, granted his request.) Then receive your sight; your faith has made you well.*

And it happened, just like Jesus said. Did scales fall from his eyes or were new eyes made where empty sockets once were? Either way, he could physically see.

Imagine it! The first thing he sees is the face of the Son of God!

Did the people gasp with surprise as the beggar turned toward them? The poor, blind crowd—having no idea who this Nazarene really was—awestruck and amazed as they stared at the blind man who stared right back at them.

I reread Eric's story about Zan. I continue to think about the blind beggar. I am still moved by the fact that Jesus, this time, overlooks those who push their way to the front. He chooses the one in the back. Because compassion is who He is. Because mercy is what He does.

I write this to Eric in a note.

He writes back and says:

You make me think of my old friend Mark and his daughter Emmy. Do you remember them? I wrote an article for the church newsletter when Emmy turned 25. I am sending it along. It's all the same story: The first are still last and the last are still first in the kingdom of God! Enjoy!

Attached was his article.

Celebrating Emmy's 25th Birthday
Church Newsletter, May 1997

    We met at Ruby Tuesdays. "It's Emmy's favorite restaurant!" Mark said with a smile.

    I've wanted to write Mark's story ever since I heard it nearly three years ago. For whatever reason, I never got around to it. But now, on the eve of Emmy's 25th birthday, I realized it was time.

    "Judy and I were married thirty-one years ago this August on Cape Cod," Mark started. Emmy was sitting

right next to him in her wheelchair. "Back then, we had no place for God in our lives. Judy was a nurse, and I was an accountant like my father. We didn't have any big dreams. Just be happy and enjoy life."

At the mention of Judy, Emmy smiled and said, "Mama!" Mark gave her a sip of Coke and told her Mama was working at the hospital.

"Emmy came along six years later. We were told we couldn't have children. So Emmy was a surprise. A good surprise! I can't tell you how excited we were. Judy had a fairly easy pregnancy."

"Did you know about Emmy's condition?" I asked.

"Not until she was born."

"What was that like?"

"We immediately knew something was wrong. The doctors whisked her away. A little while later, they told us she had a life-threatening defect in her heart that affected her lungs and breathing. On top of that, they said she had CP (cerebral palsy), and was most likely blind and deaf. They weren't sure she'd make it."

Just then, a big plate of french fries landed in front of Emmy, who squealed with delight.

"I'd never really prayed before," Mark said as he fed Emmy her fries. "But it came naturally. I started begging for her life—and to ask, at the very least—for her to see. I could handle the rest, but not that. I needed her to see us."

His voice faded as tears filled his eyes.

"We were in the hospital for three weeks. Eventually, they surgically corrected her heart issue and, after a few weeks home, we realized Emmy could hear."

"Hear and sing!" I interrupted. Who can forget Emmy's face when she sings? It's like a bright light from heaven!

"But she couldn't see," Mark said emphatically. "Everything inside of me cried out to God. So, one night, when she was six months old, I couldn't sleep. I went and scooped her out of her crib, held her in my arms, and begged God to heal her eyes. The next night, I did same thing. And the next night after."

Mark shook his head, still amazed by it all.

"On the fourth night, I suddenly saw her looking at me. I moved to the left and her eyes moved with me. Then to the right, and she did it again."

"And you knew . . ." I said.

"Yes, she could see! God had answered my prayers. A few weeks later, Judy and I went to church for the first time. Not long after, we gave our lives to Christ. The pastor let me share my story with the congregation, and all I could say was, 'First, He opened the eyes of our daughter. Then He opened our eyes, too.'"

Emmy clapped her hands right on cue.

"It's a simple story," Mark said, looking straight at me. "Emmy is the best gift God could ever give us. She brought Jesus into our lives. She taught us—and still does—that kindness is who God is and kindness is who He wants us to become."

QUESTIONS FOR REFLECTION

The blind man had faith. The eyes of his heart could see Jesus (see Eph. 1:18). What changes for you if you daily prayed this prayer?

What are your stories like this? When an answer to prayer (like the healing of Emmy's eyes) led you deeper in commitment to Jesus Christ?

8

CLOAK-FREE

Reflections on Mark 10:50 and Luke 18:43

*Throwing aside his cloak. . . . Immediately he regained
his sight and began following Him, glorifying God;
and when all the people saw it, they gave praise to God.*

—MARK 10:50; LUKE 18:43

Did he leap into the air?

*As he glorified God, did he dance? Did he know how to
dance? What Jew doesn't know how to dance? And dance with
joy! It's part of the culture. It's common life at all celebrations. It's
what King David did before the ark "with all his might." Same with
Miriam on the banks of the Red Sea (see 2 Sam. 6:14; Ex. 15:20).
Yet if he was blind from birth, how could he know?*

*And what was it like for his new eyes to take it all in—the sun
and clouds, the stunned faces in the crowd, perhaps even the
delight on Jesus' face? As he lifted his voice in praise, did he
sing? Did he praise God with that ancient song?*

*Did he shout—his voice at full strength, "I can see! I can
see!"?*

*And did the people, as they praised God with him, break into
applause and cheers? Did they clap in joy? Did they shout praises
to God and join him in song?*

*At some point, everyone's focus turned back to Jesus. He
had done what no one had ever done (see John 9:32)—He made*

the blind see! And soon enough, He started walking again. The crowd moved with Him. So did the beggar. He was following Him now—perhaps still singing, still leaping into the sky with no thought that he'd forgotten the one thing in life he owned.

It just lay there, lifeless and still, all balled up in a heap and trampled down as the crowd passed over it. His cloak—buried in the dust—just like his old life.

The picture of what was.

Never again would he come to that horrible office on the side of the road, spread out that dirty old cloak, and beg for mercy. Never again would he hear people call him "beggar" or "blind." Instead, he would be honored in the streets and in the market-places, in the synagogues and at the city gate. For he would be known as the one on whom God had mercy. And though Luke did not tell us his name, we know all we need to know about him.

He followed Jesus now. Everywhere He went. Cloak-free.

Erilynne and I got to the dinner fifteen minutes late. Eric and Missy had invited us to sit at their table for the local rescue mission fund-raiser. Cliff and Lydia were also at our table, along with two other couples.

The banquet hall was packed—some six hundred people, Eric told me.

For the last ten years or so, Cliff and Eric have spent most of their Saturday mornings down at the rescue mission. They share a love for the men who've come off the streets or out of prison, once addicted to alcohol and drugs, most coming from a poor, violent, and destructive way of life.

"What do you do with the men on Saturdays?" I once asked Eric.

"We always start with Bible study and prayer. The rest of the time, we hang out with them. Some days it's nothing more than that. Other days, some may want counseling or one-on-one time, that sort of thing. What matters is that Cliff and I are consistent. It's the only way to build trust. Every Saturday—one or both of us. That's what makes it work."

The evening was spectacular—great dinner with engaging presentations.

Surprisingly, the director of the mission rose to the microphone, turned to our table, and said, "Eric, come on up here and give the closing prayer, would you?" Eric didn't hesitate. He rose from his seat and made his way to the front.

"Ladies and gentlemen," the director announced, "this is a man who has given every Saturday morning for the last ten years to the men of the mission!"

He made no mention of Cliff whatsoever.

Eric immediately grabbed the microphone and asked people to pray with him. He was brilliant. He took the attention away from himself and pointed us to Jesus as he ended the prayer saying, "You hear the cries of the lowly and hurting, the beaten down and brokenhearted. To You, O Lord, belongs the glory and praise for Your mercy and favor are from everlasting. Now bless us, we pray, in the name of Jesus our Lord. Amen."

The director then announced, "Let's hear it for Eric!"

And with that, the crowd rose to their feet with thunderous applause. From the corner of my eye, I saw Cliff and Lydia bolt quickly from the table.

"Where are they?" Eric motioned when he got back.

I shook my head and mouthed back, "I don't know."

The next day, Eric texted me saying, **Pray for Cliff. What happened last night really hurt him.** A week later, Eric wrote me the following:

So what was the fund-raiser like for me, hearing all that applause?

Picture an alcoholic binge drinking after eleven years sober. How does that sound? Back in the day, I longed for that kind of attention. It was my addiction, my drug of choice.

But now?

You should have seen the men the following Saturday morning. Half of them were at the fund-raiser. They saw what happened. They could barely look at me. As far as they're concerned, I'm in this for me, not them. I'm out there saying, "Hey, everybody, look what I do! I help those poor wretches down at the mission!" I tell you this, those three minutes of applause cost me their trust.

And in case you're wondering, no, Cliff wasn't there. He's not talking to me right now. He sent me a quick text a few days after the dinner: **I need time. I won't be there this Saturday but next. Tell the men.**

He's angry with me, and rightly so.

I should have stopped it. I should have asked Cliff to come up and explain to the crowd that we're not in this for us. Not the recognition. Not the applause. But instead—like the beggar I was, the beggar I am—I let it happen. I basked in the praise with sheer delight. God forgive me.

And ever since, I can feel the enjoyment of that praise still filling my heart. Do you understand? I feel like I'm right back where I started. Me and the beggar. Me and my old, beat-up cloak held out for the world to see. I'm begging again. I want more. I need more. And I won't be happy until I have more.

That's the old me. It feels like the real me right now.

I need His mercy again. I want to feel what the beggar felt when the Lord gave him new eyes. He leapt. He praised. He glorified God. I want that back in my life. I want Cliff back at my side. I want the men to trust me again.

Cloak-free—that's what I want. And following Jesus wherever He goes.

Pray for me . . .

QUESTIONS FOR REFLECTION

Consider the beggar's cloak left behind in the dust. What have you thrown aside to follow Jesus?

Has it ever come back? Have you ever experienced what Eric experienced? Are you cloak-free today? Are you ready to follow Jesus wherever He goes?

PART 2

YOU
WICKED SLAVE

9

A ZILLION AND MORE

Reflections on Matthew 18:23–24

For this reason the kingdom of heaven may be compared
to a king who wished to settle accounts with his slaves.
When he had begun to settle them, one who owed
him ten thousand talents was brought to him.

—MATTHEW 18:23–24

I love our Lord's parables. They are true-to-life stories about
true-to-life people but embellished with color, drama, and a surprise
zinger at the end that leaves us closer to God.

The man who owed the money in this parable? I met someone
like this once.

He was in his late sixties. He called himself a developer. By
the age of sixteen, he'd started building his first home. Two years
later he sold it for a profit. Before it sold, he'd already contracted
friends to start a second home. And a third.

He never looked back.

Homes, apartment buildings, strip malls, corporate offices—
he did it all. Some he built and sold. Others he kept and rented.
But it never satisfied. He had to build more, build bigger. To do
that, he needed money. He needed investors. He needed loans
from banks. He needed more, always more. He never had enough.

It made life hard. Contractors were always right in his face,
hot and angry, demanding payment for their work. He fought
back as hard as they fought him, paying some, not paying others,

paying half with promises he knew—they knew—he'd never keep. He cried cash poor because he was cash poor. But no one believed him. He owned too much. He lived too well.

He made them suffer.

One of the contractors lived down the street from me. He can't pay his bills this month, nor can he help the men who work with him. They did a job for two months and got paid for two weeks. The developer told him not to worry, "I promise I'll pay you!" But hasn't. He won't. Now my neighbor has to borrow money to buy groceries for his family. The men he works with have to do the same. They're angry, all of them.

But the developer isn't upset. Somehow, he sleeps at night.

He doesn't care about the people he's cheated for the past fifty years. He doesn't even care that he owes investors and banks more money than his actual net worth. All he cares about is signing the next multi-million-dollar contract.

He has no clue that this time it won't happen.

Down at the tax office, somebody's finally figured him out. They're auditing him for back taxes. He owes, and owes big. Millions from last year. Millions more from the year before. Then back another year and another.

Truth be told, his sins go back ten, twenty, and fifty years. And if someone added it all up? Compounded by interest? What he owes the banks? What he owes all the workers he's cheated for five decades? What he'd owe if everything came into the light of day?

It's incalculable.

When Jesus told the parable, He simply called it "a zillion and more."[1]

The funeral service went on for three long hours. It was a hot summer night in the city, and the air conditioning system clearly couldn't handle a full church. As hard as it was to believe, people stood, lining the walls, the entire time.

Up front, their well-loved pastor lay in an open casket.

The service was nothing less than a wild ride of emotion. After thirty years at the church, in his midsixties, robust and full of energy, the pastor simply died in his sleep. "Around here, we call this a 'home-going'!" a young minister said as he started the service. "Though we grieve our pastor's death, we are here to celebrate his entrance into glory. I want you to sing, I want you to praise God tonight!" Right on cue, the choir rose, the music roared, and the place filled with an almost ecstatic joy.

An hour later, it seemed like everybody was crying.

It started as the mayor gave his remarks. It increased incrementally as an endless line of dignitaries rose to the microphone to give their eulogies. As an outsider, I felt like some were just stirring the crowd's emotions.

After the service, I stood in line to greet the family. The woman in front of me could see I was a visitor. "Most funerals at our church aren't like this," she offered, almost apologetically. "Tonight was different. Maybe it's because we're all in shock." I nodded and told her I was sorry for her loss.

"I'm here to see Ricky," I said, making conversation.

"Ricky?" she frowned, disapprovingly. I could tell she wanted to ask why but didn't. Instead, she warned under her breath, "You be careful of that one." I nodded, understanding her concern.

I volunteer at a men's recovery program a couple of times a month. I'd seen Ricky only twice. He'd just been released from prison. He was there maybe two weeks before being transferred to a program upstate.

"Can I have your cell number?" he insisted the first day we met.

I'd been sitting with him and a handful of guys in the cafeteria. We were just talking like we always do. He leaned toward me with a serious look on his face. "Do you mind if I call you once in a while? Maybe you could pray for me?"

"Tell me your name again," I said as I wrote my number on a piece of paper.

"Richard," he said, "but they call me Ricky." In the few minutes we talked, I realized he was asking me to be on his recovery team. "Will you pray for me every day, Pastor?" I could see it in his eyes. He wanted me to remember him, to know his name, and to go before God and fight for him to make it in this world. "Do you promise?" he said with surprising urgency.

I didn't hesitate. I promised him.

We talked a couple of times a year. He'd call, I'd call, and it was always the same thing. "I don't want to take your time, Pastor," he'd begin. "All I want is for you to pray for me on the phone. Will you do that?" I knew next to nothing about him, and he didn't seem to care. All he wanted was for me to pray for him every day. Only once did he ask for more. And that happened a few days ago.

"My dad died last night," he said. "I was wondering if you could come to his funeral service this Sunday night at our church."

I told him I wouldn't miss it.

When he saw me in line, he bolted for me and hugged me like a long lost friend. "I gotta meet with you," he said. "Soon, real soon." He was now living in the area. We settled on Friday lunch at a local diner. I told him I was sorry about his dad.

"Yeah, whatever," he shrugged, his eyes looking back at the casket. "I'm just glad you came. It means a lot to me."

In that one expression, as he looked back at his dad, I saw there was a world of hurt inside him. I hoped then, when we met for lunch, he'd finally tell me his story. I couldn't help but wonder how he ended up in prison, especially growing up as a pastor's son. Something had happened to him, but what?

A few days later, I got a handwritten letter in the mail with no return address.

Pastor,

Gotta tell you some things before we meet Friday.

I was a good boy growing up, mostly because of my grandmother. She watched over me. She made sure I got to school and stayed in school. And I did well. I was smart. She always sat next to me in church and made sure I knew my Bible. She prayed for me. My dad didn't. He couldn't care. I think my mama was too scared of my dad to help any of us kids much. I'm pretty sure my grandmother knew that and did the best she could with us.

She died when I was about thirteen. I went bad after that. Did my first jail time a year later—burglary and assault. Back to jail when I was sixteen for drugs. Two more times before I hit twenty. I kept telling myself it was the drugs. But I knew better. I was angry. I hated my dad. I hated that the man I saw in church wasn't the man I saw at home. I hated what he did to my mother. I left school. I hit the streets and never looked back.

Pastor, you need to know what kind of man I am.

When I turned twenty-one, a couple of us did a hit on a liquor store. The man fought back and I hit him, hit him hard, and this rage took over. I couldn't stop hitting him. By the time my buddies pulled me off him it was too late. The police were already there. I was handcuffed, thrown into prison, and charged with robbery, assault, and murder.

I killed the man.

You still want to meet with me? It's OK if you don't.

Ricky

QUESTIONS FOR REFLECTION

This parable is set in a conversation on forgiveness (see Matt. 18:21–22). Why, in order to know His mercy, does our Lord want us to see the depth of our debt?

Do you compare your debt with others? Is yours more manageable than Ricky's? How have you ever felt more worthy than others to receive His mercy?

NOTE

1. In R. T. France's commentary *The Gospel of Matthew* ([Grand Rapids, MI: Eerdmans, 2007], 706), he explains that one denarius equals a day's labor (see Matt. 20:2). Six thousand denarii (roughly twenty years of labor if working three hundred days a year) equals one talent. Ten thousand talents, therefore, equals sixty million denarii and, therefore, some two hundred thousand years of labor. The effect to the hearers is to put this man's debt (and, therefore, ours) infinitely beyond comparison. In our modern-day language, France says, it "is like our zillions."

10

EXPOSED

~~~

Reflections on Matthew 18:24–26

When he had begun to settle them, one who owed him ten thousand talents was brought to him. But since he did not have the means to repay, his lord commanded him to be sold, along with his wife and children and all that he had, and repayment to be made. So the slave fell to the ground.

—MATTHEW 18:24–26

It's not often we see a great man, an elite member of society, standing before a judge in the highest courtroom in the land. But that's the story here.

It's about a man, a wealthy man, summoned by his king.

I wonder what the wealthy man thought when he was first summoned. Did the king's police come for him? Is it possible he had no idea why they'd come? Was his mind so drunk in self-deceit he couldn't even think what he'd done wrong?

It's possible, isn't it? For him, for us.

Did he laugh under his breath when he heard the charges? Did he get that smug, arrogant look on his face? Did he have lawyers at his beck and call? Perhaps he trusted them a little too much. Perhaps he thought he'd be home by nightfall. Did he say it out loud: "You have no idea who you're dealing with"?

Were his lawyers the first to break the news: "There's nothing we can do. What they say you owe, you owe"? Is it possible his legal team walked out on him and left him standing alone before the king, completely exposed and without legal defense? When did he finally *understand he was not invincible? And what was it like when the king spoke to him as if he was nothing more than a "slave"?*

Poor man. Jesus gave him no other name.

The king had obviously been told how much this slave owed, perhaps in detail. Did it take time for the king to explain it all to him? And what was it like when his slave finally heard the exact amount? Did he say, "What? How much do I owe?"

The king then immediately demanded full and immediate repayment.

But the slave couldn't do it and told the king he had no means to repay.

Upon hearing this, the king commanded, by royal decree, that his police seize the slave, his wife and children, and all they owned. Everything was to be sold—including the family into slavery—for as long as it would take for repayment to be made in full.[1]

At the sound of the king's voice, the man crumpled to the ground.

It's not every day I go to lunch with a convicted murderer. But for me, that day, I couldn't wait to see Ricky—and we talked like two old friends who knew each other better than we did. As the time passed, I kept wondering why he wanted to meet with me. Was it just to get to know each other, or did he have something else in mind? I couldn't help but think it was related to his dad's death somehow but I didn't know.

Then suddenly, stopping mid-sentence, he leaned back in his chair and said, "Pastor, I can't believe you're here. Not after I sent that letter."

"It didn't change things for me."

"You mean that?"

"Yeah, I do. Plus, I've been concerned for you since your father passed."

He reached for a bunch of papers beside him and said, "I want to talk to you about my dad, but first I have to tell you about my two daughters. Esther, she's twenty-two and has two kids. Did you know I was a grandfather?" That ear-to-ear smile came back as he reached for his wallet to show me pictures. "Then there's Dora, she's twenty, and had her first child three months ago."

He pointed to each one, naming his grandchildren.

I asked if he had a good relationship with them. "Kind of," he said as he tucked his wallet back in his jeans. "But that's why I want to talk. God has put it on my heart to write my story. I have to. The girls need to know the truth about what their dad did and what kind of man I am. But every time I talk with them . . ."

His voice broke. He turned his head away.

"They don't want to hear it, huh?" I said, trying to finish his thought. He shook his head, rubbed his eyes, and started to shuffle through the stack of papers. "I was hoping you could help me do this. Maybe clean it up a bit," he said. "My grammar stinks. Same with my spelling. My hand-writing's a mess." He kept rifling through his papers like he was looking for something in particular.

"Yeah, I'd love to."

"Here it is," he said. He handed me a couple of pages. "I want you to read this part first and see what you think." I took it from him and said I would.

"By this point in the story," he began, "I've already done my time for murder. Supposed to serve twenty-five years. Got out in half that time."

"Why didn't you get a life sentence?"

"The judge ruled it wasn't premeditated. Otherwise, I'd still be there. So, for me, I knew if I did things right, if I did my work, kept to myself, took classes, and didn't mess up, I'd be up for parole and get out early. Which I did. A week later, I got a job, found a place to live, and landed on my feet. This time, I swore I'd stay clean and never look back."

"Was God in your life at that point?"

He shook his head and said, "I wanted nothing to do with Him."

"So what happened?"

"About a year later, I went back to drugs. Next thing I know, the cops are banging down my door and arresting me for assault. I was so drugged out I had no memory of what I'd done. They said I beat up my cousin so bad I put him in the hospital. They handcuffed me and took me out of my house. And guess who's standing outside on the street watching the whole thing?"

"Your girls?"

"You got it. And that's where this part of the story picks up," he said, pointing to the pages in my hand. I looked down at his handwriting, sipped my coffee, and began to read as Ricky sat back in his chair and stared out the window.

I hated you saw all that.

"I didn't do it!" I screamed at you both. "Do you hear me? I didn't do it!"

And then Esther stepped forward and told me, "Daddy, we were there. We saw it all."

I couldn't sleep that night in jail. The look on your faces—you seeing me like that—was too much for me. Inside, I wanted to lie to you like I lie to myself.

"It's not my fault," I wanted to tell you. "My father did this to me, do you get it?"

But that night, seeing you see me, changed all that. It's like it all came down on me, everything I've ever done. It was all my fault—the drugs, the things I've stolen, the people I've hurt, the women I've loved and hurt—including your mom—my fault, no one else's. And it was my fault for the man I killed.

It's like that night, for the first time, I saw that man's face again. I saw his wife and two boys sitting in the courtroom at the trial. I saw it all—everyone looking at me like you two were that night when I was arrested.

Even my grandmother. It's like I could see her seeing me too—and doing what she always did, pointing me to God and telling me He could see too.

Like you two did.

It all came down that night. All of it—my fault— for the first time in my life I knew it. I could own it. And when I did, all I could do was cry.

QUESTIONS FOR REFLECTION

What if, today, you were summoned to stand before your King? Are you ready? Are you wrestling with self-deceit? When have you felt exposed?

Has what happened to Ricky—coming face-to-face with his sin—ever happened to you? When did you know God can see you too (see Heb. 4:13)?

NOTE

1. The reader is left with the obvious conclusion that one lifetime, let alone a thousand lifetimes, could not even begin to repay the enormity of this man's debt—and, by implication, our debt as well.

11
GIVE ME A CHANCE

Reflections on Matthew 18:26

*The poor wretch threw himself at the king's feet
and begged, "Give me a chance and I'll pay it all back."*

—MATTHEW 18:26 MSG

It happens a lot.

The moment judgment is pronounced, the guilty almost always cry for mercy. They beg the court for leniency as if, in a last-ditch effort, they'll be heard. Their voice usually gets louder as they're taken away—desperately louder. The doors open, the doors close, and their muffled voice trails off until, at last, it's gone.

But this one was different.

This one fell humbly at the king's feet and somehow won his attention. Was it because he refused to lift his head and look into the king's face? Or was it because he didn't do what a lot of them did and still do. He didn't cry foul saying he was innocent that he didn't do what people say he did, or didn't mean to, or didn't deserve to be sentenced like that.

Not him. His voice, his posture, even his words confessed that he was a broken, guilty man. Perhaps this alone made the king stretch forth his hand, stopping the police from grabbing him and hauling him away.

The small voice said, "Give me a chance."

It doesn't seem possible that the king would listen to the poor wretch. After all, he was nothing more than a thief, and what thief ever had a voice in his kingdom? Weren't they regarded as mere property—like animals—expelled from the rank and dignity of even being called human?

"I will pay it all back—everything."

One flick of the king's hand and the police would descend on him immediately. One flick and it would have been over. But instead, the king decided to hear the man's plea. Is it possible this slave actually thought it was possible to negotiate the absolutely impossible?

Did he really think he could pay back everything?

The king stood there reflecting on the request. Perhaps every eye was fixed on him wondering why he hadn't banished the thief already. Maybe the crowd in the courtroom expected it, especially for what this man had done. But still the king didn't move. Was he actually considering it?

That small sound, perhaps it came again. Slowly, quietly.

"Give me a chance . . ."

"This is beautiful," I said to Ricky, handing the papers back to him. "I mean, really well done. You're giving your daughters your heart." A waitress came by, poured more coffee, and put the check on the table.

"Thanks, but it needs work."

"Not much from what I can tell." I watched him drizzle cream and sugar in his coffee and stir it. "Have you finished writing it?"

"Not yet. I haven't written the part about my father. My girls have to know the whole story. The men in my family have messed up for generations, and I have to break the cycle. It ends with me. I don't want it touching my grandkids. If my daughters can see it, they can do something about it."

"Tell me about your dad."

"Mind if I hold off on that for a bit more? I'd much rather tell you what happened next, after that night in the jail cell."

"Yeah, of course," I said, not wanting to rush him.

"There was a Bible in the cell. I picked it up and started reading. I can't tell you how it happened, but it's like I already knew what was in it. Most of what my grandmother taught me came back to me that night. Whatever she planted in my soul, it's like it came to life. I'm telling you, before the sun came up the next morning, I knew I was saved. I knew I'd serve out my sentence and that'd be it. I'd never be coming back to jail—ever."

He stopped, his smile came back, his look turned confident. "Oh, thank You, Jesus! Just remembering that night makes me praise Him!"

I smiled back, echoing his thanks.

"The guys in prison knew something was different too. They'd come to me, spilling their guts, asking me to pray for them, and I did. It's like God had favor on me. He let me do for others like He was doing for me. I'm telling you, I saw miracles, prayers answered. Some of the guys were saved. I was there a couple of months, and it was the best time of my life in a long time. I almost didn't want to leave, but when I did, I came out a new man. I was never going to be what I was."

He reached out and tapped my hand.

"That's when you and I met. Remember that?" Ricky said, pointing at me. "And I asked you to pray for me. Man, I needed prayer. I hadn't seen my daughters yet, not since the day they saw me arrested in front of my house. I was so scared. I was afraid they wouldn't want to see me, let alone talk to me."

Again, Ricky turned his face toward the window. I could tell this part wasn't easy for him to relive.

"The Lord helped me. I said to Esther and Dora, 'I know you're not going to believe me. But something happened to me in prison. The Lord did something in my life. If I'm right about that, if I've changed, you'll know it someday. Not because I'm saying it but because I'm living it. All I ask is that you pray for me.'

"But they wanted nothing to do with me. They were hurt—hurt bad. So I made up my mind to do the best I could. I went to rehab upstate. When I got out, I found a job, found a place to live, and started going back to church. The pastor of my church is a good man. He promised to come alongside and help me."

Ricky picked up the stack of papers and said, "And you can read the rest."

"Hey, that's not fair. You have to finish the story!" I teased.

He got that Ricky smile again, ear to ear. "I gotta go." He grabbed the check and went to the counter to pay for it. "If you don't mind," he said when he got back, "do what you can to make the letter read better. I'll try to finish it before we meet again."

We set a date for two weeks later—same time, same place—and said our good-byes.

As I walked to the car, I kept looking at this letter in my hand, a long letter, maybe thirty handwritten pages, front and back. I found the place where he'd ended his story and, once in the car, I started reading. As always, Ricky surprised me. What I thought was coming next wasn't coming at all.

Not yet anyway.

If I wasn't working or at home sleeping, I was at church. I wanted to be there to help out, clean up, and do work projects on the building. I was there for every service. I'd made up my mind—I was gonna live my life for God.

One day, the pastor looked at me said, "Why are you always here?"

"I feel like God wants me here," I told him.

"Are you doing what you do for Him or for you?" he asked.

"What kind of question is that?" I asked back. "I'm here for Him!"

"You sure? You think about it and get back to me," he said and walked away. That really bothered me. I prayed about it for a few days. I finally asked God, "Lord, maybe I'm trying to prove myself to my daughters. Is that it? Is that why I'm doing all this?" I finally went to my pastor and asked him to explain it to me.

"Maybe that, maybe not," he said.

"What else could it be?"

"Could be guilt for what you've done. Guilt for the people you hurt. Guilt for the man you killed and the family he left behind. Guilt for the father you hate. Guilt for what you've done to your family. Guilt for all the sins you've done to God. Guilt that piles up as high as the mountains and pushes the soul down into hell."

I hate it when I cry. The older I get, the more it happens. But for me, it almost always happens when I feel like God is speaking to me. And, right then, I started to cry in front of the pastor.

"You're trying to pay it back, Ricky. Pay it all back. That's what I think."

"Yes, sir, I'm doing my best, sir," I told him, wiping my eyes. "You've got to believe me, I'm doing my best."

QUESTIONS FOR REFLECTION

What makes us say what this slave said: "Give me a chance and I'll pay it all back"? Why do we think we can negotiate the impossible?

Consider the pastor's insight for your life: Is guilt driving you? When have you tried hard to please God so you can pay Him back for the mercy you have received?

12

KINDNESS BEYOND IMAGINING

Reflections on Matthew 18:27

*And the lord of that slave felt compassion and
released him and forgave him the debt.*

—MATTHEW 18:27

I imagine a reporter on the steps of the king's palace: "Tell
us what happened!"

A man answers, "I wasn't in the king's chamber. I was standing
outside when we heard a sudden burst of applause. When the
doors finally opened, people were saying the king showed mercy
to a man who owed an outrageous debt! I know nothing more. I
never heard the man's story."

"I did," someone snaps in anger. "This guy owed more money
than what our country makes in fifty years.[1] He begged the king
for time to pay it back. Can you imagine that? And get this, the
king granted his request. It's not fair!"

"Why isn't it fair?" the reporter presses.

"If you ask me, the king should've put country first. We can't
afford not to have that money and have it now."

One of the king's policemen standing in earshot shakes his
head and says, "That's not what happened."

"Were you there?"

"Only a few feet away."

"What did you see?"

"Like nothing I've ever seen before. Usually when the king renders judgment, we remove the person from the chamber. But this time he commanded us to step back. He wanted to hear what the man had to say. I saw compassion in the king's eyes, tenderness like a father would have for his own child. Even then, I didn't think he'd change his mind. But he did."

"What do you mean?" the reporter asks.

"The poor man was scared to death, afraid to even lift his head. The king then spoke barely above a whisper, and said, 'I will not grant your request to pay me back. Do you hear me?' The man nodded, still refusing to look at him. 'Instead, I will do more than you can ever imagine. Today, in your hearing, I release you from your debt. Everything you owe me, from now on, is paid in full. Do you understand?'

"Those of us who heard the king gasped. We couldn't believe our ears. Neither could the man. He raised his head and whispered back, 'What was that?'

"'I forgive it all,' the king repeated. 'Now go, pay what you owe others. Show mercy as I have shown you mercy, and from now on, do what is right by me.' With that, a trumpet sounded and a loud voice announced, 'The king has forgiven the man his debt! He has shown mercy!' and the whole place erupted in applause."

The policeman says it again, this time for everyone outside the palace to hear, "The king has shown mercy!" And with that, the crowd around him burst into a rousing cheer.

Later that night, I picked up Ricky's letter to his daughters and kept reading.

A few months passed. I still hadn't figured out what the pastor was saying. I kept working myself to the bone—at work and at church. I was happy most of the time but, if I were to be honest, I missed you girls more than I can say. I kept praying, "Lord, be with my daughters. Don't let what I've done get in their way."

One Saturday afternoon, I was working in the church yard when the pastor walked over and said, "Still haven't figured it out yet, have you, Ricky?" I didn't know what to tell him. Then he said, "You got it, you know you got it, but you won't receive it. Now tell me why?"

"Pastor, I'm doing what I can," I said, upset.

"You tell me Jesus saved you, is that right?" he asked, obviously concerned for me.

"Yes, sir."

"Well, what's that mean to you, Ricky?"

"It means I'm a different man. I'm not like what I was."

"But tell me what He saved you from."

"From my sins."

"All of them, Ricky?"

"Yes, sir."

"Well then, receive it. When Jesus died on the cross, He took away your sin. He took away the guilt of your sin. He took away the power of your sin. He took it all, you hear me? You gotta stop paying back what He already paid. If you're forgiven by Jesus, be forgiven, live forgiven. Something's gotta change, Ricky."

I stood there, shaking my head. "What am I supposed to do?"

"Ask Him to make it real to you. And when He does, receive it."

"Pastor, I'm gonna live with the guilt of what I've done all my life. You know that. You know there's no getting around it. I can't take back what I've done."

"Ricky, you're not listening to me. I'm telling you, it's over. You got that?"

When I heard him say, "It's over," I got down on my knees and asked him to pray for me. I asked the Lord to forgive me. I didn't mean to insult Him by doing what He'd already done. I gave Him my guilt. Now, it didn't happen right away. It took some time. But eventually the Lord helped me understand. And when I did, things changed for me. I went back to my pastor and he gave me the best counsel.

He said, "Ricky, you did what you did out of guilt. Now go do what you do out of love. He showed you mercy; go show mercy. He showed you kindness; go be kind. He showed you blessing; now be a blessing. Give what He gave you and never stop because—thank You, Jesus—He did it all! It's paid! We get to love as we've been loved. We get to forgive like we've been forgiven. You're free, Ricky."

And I was. I knew it.

So I started asking the Lord what He wanted me to do. Where do I start? First thing I did was pray for the widow of the man I killed. One thing led to another and

I learned she was attending a Pentecostal church across town. So I decided to go to that church and meet with her pastor. One day, I just walked into the church office and asked if I could see him. I was told to come back later that afternoon.

So I did. I met with him. I told him my story, every bit of it. I told him I'd come to see if there was anything I could do for her.

"I'll tell her you came by and asked for her," he assured me. "I'll tell her what the Lord has done for you. She'll want to know that. She thinks you're still in prison, you know. It'll be hard for her to hear that you're not. But when she comes to terms with it, I think she'll be glad to know the man who murdered her husband isn't out there murdering others. He's walking with the Lord now."

"Will you tell her I'm sorry, and I'm praying for her and her family?"

The pastor agreed and asked, "So what's next for you, Ricky?" I told him I didn't know. And then he asked the strangest question. He said, "Are you right with your family, Ricky? That's where it all starts, you know."

I nodded my head. But I got this ache in my heart. I suddenly knew what he meant. If the Lord showed me mercy, was I ready to show mercy to the one man I hated most in my life? I knew the answer. But nothing inside me wanted to do it. But there, in that pastor's office, I promised him I would.

And I knew—it was time to deal with my dad.

QUESTIONS FOR REFLECTION

What does the King's mercy mean to you? What is it like for your heart to hear, "Paid in full" and "I forgive it all"?

What things prevent you from receiving the mercy of God given to you at Calvary's hill? What does it mean to live in the freedom of that mercy?

NOTE

1. Again, in France's commentary on Matthew, he records that the ancient historian Josephus reported "the total annual tax income from the whole of Galilee and Perea in 4 BC was only two hundred talents." At this rate, it would take fifty years to raise the ten thousand talents. (R. T. France, *The Gospel of Matthew* [Grand Rapids, MI: Eerdmans, 2007], 706, note 22.)

13
THE LION ROARED

Reflections on Matthew 18:28–31

*So when his fellow slaves saw what had happened,
they were deeply grieved and came and reported
to their lord all that had happened.*

—MATTHEW 18:31

I wonder how these men got access to the king. As "fellow slaves," as peers to the man who'd been forgiven, they'd have had money too. They'd have had stature. Perhaps they were nobles. Perhaps they were the kind of people who were invited to sit at the king's banquet table on occasion and, maybe, that's how it happened.

I imagine a dinner at the king's table.

"Tell me, nobles, why do you all look so troubled?" Perhaps these men were sitting together, talking, whispering. The king's voice may have startled them.

"Please, your Majesty, we don't want to concern you," one of them says.

"You must. I insist. You all appear terribly sad. Has someone you love died?" Almost in unison, they dropped their heads, not wanting to speak. I imagine the king, perceiving their sorrow, saying calmly, "What can I do to help?"

"We bear sad news today, my lord," the elder statesman among them replies. "On our way here, as we passed the city gate, we witnessed a crime of unspeakable violence by a man who is our colleague."

"Tell me," the king invites.

"You remember a few weeks ago," the nobleman continues, "you summoned a man into your chamber. He owed you the greatest of all debts. He had no means to repay and so, by royal edict, you sold him and his family into slavery."

"Go on," he says, interested.

"You had compassion on him, my lord. We saw it. We were there."

"But tonight," another says, continuing the story, "we saw him fighting at the city gate. He'd seized a man by the throat. We rushed to the scene to see what we could do. But the police arrived at the same time. Our colleague was choking the man violently and without mercy, shouting, 'Pay back what you owe. You hear me? Pay back what you owe.' The police intervened and broke it up.

"The man, gasping for breath, fell down and begged for mercy. He said, 'Have patience with me; I'll repay you'—nearly the same words, my lord, our colleague spoke to you. But our colleague had no mercy in his soul. He produced proof of the debt owed him and ordered the police to throw the man in jail until all is repaid."

"It was not an insignificant debt," another one of them adds. "For a common worker, he owed four months' salary. I believe it's why the police arrested him."

The king's face burns hot with anger.

"We went straight to our colleague and demanded that he release the prisoner. We pleaded with him: 'You can't do this. As the king showed mercy to you, you must show mercy to him. What will the king do when he hears about this?'

"'And how will the king,' he said, laughing at us, 'ever find out?'"

With that, the king threw back his head and roared. Seconds later, guards were at his side. He quickly dispatched them—for *the second time that month—to the home of the man upon whom he'd once shown mercy.*

"So you finished the letter?" I asked Ricky as I pointed to the papers next to him. We were back at the same diner and, oddly enough, at the same booth by the window.

"Not yet."

"Did you finish the section on your father?"

"Yeah," he said.

Again, I told him how impressed I was at the honesty of his writing. I could tell he wasn't trying to win his girls' love. Instead, he wanted to break the cycle of violence that had plagued the men in their family for generations.

"Before you read it," he said, "I want to tell you about my dad. You saw the mayor at his funeral, right? Police commissioner? State senator? He was a powerful man. All his life he fought for the rights and dignity of every African-American. In the same way, he refused to let the government ignore the city's poor. If he smelled injustice, he'd rally hundreds to march on city hall. For him, the marginalized mattered. He was their voice and champion. You mess with them, you mess with God. And every politician knew that about my dad."

"That's the impression I got at his funeral."

"Outside the home, he was heroic—traveling the world, driving the most expensive cars, wearing the most expensive clothes and jewelry. He rubbed shoulders with senators and congressmen. He got to meet the president of the United States. My dad had a name. My dad lived like a king. But inside the home? Different story, different man."

Ricky leaned in, quieting his voice, "I was scared of him growing up. You set him off—you do something wrong, say something wrong—and that was it. He'd beat us, beat us bad. My two brothers, my sister, and my mother.

"When I was fourteen, after my grandmother died, I caught him cheating on my mother—in his own house. He didn't know I knew, but the next time he went after my mother, I went after him. I pushed him back and told him to leave her alone. I told him I knew about his mistress, and all he did was laugh at me and yell, 'You ain't nothing but a piece of trash, Ricky. That's all you are, that's all you'll ever be.' After that, I left home."

"Did you ever see him again?"

"Yeah, but it's like I didn't exist. Once I started using drugs and doing jail time—it was pretty much over anyway."

"Did he stop the affair?" I asked.

"No, sir."

"Did he keep beating your mom?"

"Not as much. When he got famous, he needed her to look good," he said as he handed me the letter. "I want you to read the part when I went back to see him after I got saved. It was the hardest thing I'd ever done. I still hated him. I hated the lies, the cheating, being one man on the outside and another man on the inside and all the while telling people that Christ has the power to save. But I did it. I went to see him. Start here and see what you think."

He pointed to a spot on the paper. I sat back and began reading.

I went to church to see him. I'm not sure how it happened, but I got to his office door without being noticed. The door was open so I walked in thinking he'd be there, but he wasn't. His computer was on and there was music playing so I figured he must've stepped out for a minute. So I waited.

Made me wonder if I'd been there before. I had no memory of it. His desk, the chairs, and the leather sofa— it was all new to me. I found myself staring at an entire wall filled with framed photographs. In each one, he's standing with the most famous people in the world— celebrities, world leaders, politicians.

I was nervous before I got there. I wasn't nervous anymore.

For the first time in my life, I felt compassion in my heart for my father. Not pity, not like I felt sorry for him. I figured if the Lord had forgiven me for what I'd done, He could forgive my father for what he'd done. I wanted him to know that. I wanted him to know I loved him. I'd never stop praying for him.

And, more, I'd forgiven him.

Next thing I know, he was in the room, slamming the door behind him. As I turned to see him, his face all twisted in anger, I heard a loud, guttural roar. He came at me fast, his right arm cocked back, his fist balled up, and then I felt it slamming against the right side of my face as he hit me. I went down hard and blacked out.

When I woke up, he was gone.

QUESTIONS FOR REFLECTION

How is this slave's story possible? When has it been true of you? When, having received the gift of God's mercy in Christ, have you not shown mercy?

When are you ever like Ricky's father—one person on the outside, another on the inside? When have you ever incited the King's roar?

14

THE TORTURERS

Reflections on Matthew 18:32–34

*"You wicked slave. . . . Should you not also have had mercy on
your fellow slave, in the same way that I had mercy on you?"
And his lord, moved with anger, handed him over to the torturers.*

—MATTHEW 18:32–34

What was it like when they met again?

*Was the man allowed to come near the king? Were his hands
bound? Did the police treat him more like a criminal this time?
Was the chamber filled with the same people who saw the king
once extend his gracious mercy to him? I wonder if he was
scared.*

*Or maybe he believed the king's edict was irrevocable. If he
swore mercy, could he go back on his word? If he relieved him
of his debt, could he return his debt? Was the man perhaps a
little too confident, even smug? Or was he, in fact, trembling?*

I imagine the king reviewing the events with the crowd gathered.

*"Do you remember him? This is the man who owed me the
greatest of all debts. Didn't you see him fall at my feet and beg
for patience, for mercy? Did I not give it to him? And if I did, what
did he do with it?"*

The crowd stares at the man. The king now speaks to him.

*"I showed you mercy. Why didn't you show mercy in the
same way to the man who begged you for mercy? Instead, you*

beat him in rage. You choked him in violence. You had no patience with him. You threw him in prison. What happened to the mercy I gave you? Who stole it from your heart? Answer me!"

But there is no answer.

"Then hear this: The mercy I gave is the mercy I take back. From this day on, you will never be known as 'He upon whom the king showed favor.' We will call you by a new name, by what you are— 'Wicked Slave!'—for wicked is your heart and wicked is your soul."

With that, the king thunders, "Torturers, come!"

I imagine it all. A group of men dressed in black descending on Wicked Slave. They cover his face like Haman (see Est. 7:8). There is no mention of his wife or children. No mention of being sold into slavery. Not this time. He is dragged off alone into a land of torture where there is no mercy. The chamber doors open and close. The man is gone. And all he has are the king's last words ringing in his ears: "And there you will stay until you repay it all!"

A zillion and more.

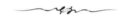

I looked at Ricky and winced.

"Took forever to stop the bleeding," Ricky said, rubbing a two-inch scar on his right brow. "My mom came over that night—she'd heard. She saw my right eye all puffed up and swollen shut. She got some more ice and sat with me for a while. I felt so bad for her. Why wasn't I there for her in the old days when he beat her? Not me, I was too self-centered. The second I was old enough to get out, I did, not even thinking about her. That night, I told her I was sorry.

"She said, 'You're here now, Ricky. That's all that matters.'

"I asked her, 'Did he say anything?'"

"She nodded, and I knew. I said, 'He doesn't want to see me again, right?' She got that look in her eyes, and real quiet, she said, 'You can't change him, Ricky. But he can change you. You hear me? Don't let him. You went that path once. Don't do it again. You gotta put your eyes on Jesus now. Don't do like you did before.'"

"It was the best thing she could've said."

"Sounds like she knows you," I observed.

"She does. I tell you, that woman knows the Lord," Ricky said proudly.

I couldn't help but ask, "Did you ever see your father again?"

"Not until he was in his casket at church."

"Do you think he changed at the end?"

"You know how he died?" he growled. I told him I'd heard he'd died in his sleep. "That's right," Ricky said. "Police say he died peacefully at home next to his wife of forty-one years. But that's not what happened. He died like he lived. The real story is he was friends with the police commissioner and the mayor."

I looked at him, puzzled. I didn't understand.

"He died in the bed of his mistress across town. They covered it up. Then at his funeral they made him look like a saint. You heard it. They even promised they'd name a street after him. They promised to start a foundation in his name, the biggest in the city's history, to give poor kids a shot at a decent education. They chose to protect my father's legacy."

"I can't believe the media didn't find out," I responded.

"They didn't. Somebody up top made sure of it."

"Do your daughters know?"

"Not sure. But they don't know it from me."

I tried to take it all in. I finally said, "Ricky, I'm so sorry. I can't imagine what this is like for you."

He nodded, reached into his pocket, pulled out a folded piece of paper, and handed it to me. He said, "I didn't write this for my girls. I wrote it for you."

It was written on simple lined paper, with handwriting I'd come to know well.

I'm having nightmares.

I see myself in a great hall surrounded by a huge crowd of people. The Lord is there, but I can't see Him. It's the best feeling in the whole world. I'm doing everything I can to catch a glimpse of Him when, off to the side, these huge doors open up and my father comes in.

He's bound in chains, encircled by guards. He's wearing his pastor's robe, but it's torn and dirty. I can see on his face that smirk I despise so much.

Then I hear this thunderous sound, "Wicked Slave!"

I don't know how I know, but I do. The Lord has just spoken. My father reels back like the words actually hit him. He turns ashen. The smirk is gone. His face is dark and ugly. The image of glory he once knew in this world has left him.

It's him now—the real him. Worse than the one we knew at home.

Again, I hear the Lord speak: "From this day on, we will call you what you are—Wicked Slave!—for wicked is your heart and wicked is your soul."

I feel my own heart pounding. I feel a deep wail ready to burst out of me. I don't want to hear what comes next. I don't want to hear the sentence passed on him and, next thing I know, the wailing comes out of me. I shoot up in bed, crying, "Dad!"

I'm awake. I'm scared.

QUESTIONS FOR REFLECTION

If this slave had received mercy, why wasn't he changed by it? How can this scenario be applied to you? At what point does the King take back His mercy?

Do you know stories of people like Ricky's dad? How do you wrestle with being one thing on the outside and something totally different on the inside?

15

WITH ALL MY HEART

Reflections on Matthew 18:35

*My heavenly Father will also do the same to you, if each
of you does not forgive his brother from your heart.*

—MATTHEW 18:35

The story was now over.

*It all started because Peter asked Jesus, "Lord, how often
shall my brother sin against me and I forgive him? Up to seven
times?" (Matt. 18:21).*

*Jesus could've simply answered, "No, Peter. Never stop,
ever," and left it at that. But instead, He told the horrifying story
of Wicked Slave. He made us see what happened to him—all
because he refused to show mercy as he was shown mercy. He
even made us see the torturers dragging him away. I don't like
this story.*

*Nor that Jesus applied it to me: "My heavenly Father will also
do the same to you, if each of you does not forgive his brother
from your heart" (Matt. 18:35).*

I picture myself back in the parable.

*After the chamber doors close and Wicked Slave is gone, I
imagine the king's anger subsiding. "It's not supposed to be this
way," he tells the crowd. "I took the debt he owed at great personal
cost to myself. I did it because it's what mercy and compassion*

do. It's the royal law of my kingdom. It is the way of my Father because it is who my Father is. Who doesn't know this?" he asks, bewildered.

Everyone remains quiet.

"Don't you know the secret? The kind of mercy my Father and I give enters and changes your heart. It comes alive in you. It becomes your teacher all the days of your life. It teaches you, even when someone hurts or offends you, to forgive as you've been forgiven, to love as you've been loved, and to treat them as I've treated you.

"But this man? I tell you, mercy never entered his heart. He despised it. Can't we see that by how he treated others?

"So, open your heart, my friends, and let my Father's mercy in. I have taken your debt too. I've paid it in full. If you receive my mercy with all your heart, it will reign inside you. You'll know it. You'll feel it. It'll burst out of you! But mark my words, if you do not, what happened here today . . . will also happen to you."

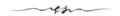

A line of tears streaked down Ricky's face. I could tell he had climbed back into the nightmare all over again, the film replaying, his emotions raw. We sat there awhile, not saying anything.

"My pastor told me to give him to Jesus," Ricky said. "What happens now is between him and the Lord. Not me and him. Not anymore. That part is done. But he warned me, 'You be careful. Don't you dare walk away from Jesus now.'"

He turned toward me as he dried his face.

"He kept saying, 'You deal straight, Ricky, you hear me? You bury hate? It'll come back. You bury resentment?

It'll come back. You bury unforgiveness? It'll come back and follow you wherever you go. What you were is what you'll become and a whole lot worse. Don't you dare walk away, Ricky.'

"'But he's dead,' I told him. 'I can't work it out with him now.'

"'Then work it out with Jesus,' he told me. 'You take your baggage of the past and lay it at the cross. That's what we do. We lay the burdens down. We lay the hate down. We lay the bitterness down. We say, "Jesus, Lord, as You forgave me, I forgive my father. You paid my debt. You did for me—so I do for him."'

"I told him, 'It makes no sense to me. What about my nightmares? You know about judgment day. You think he's getting through that?'

"'None of your business,' he said, and said it strong.

"'But if the Lord won't show him mercy now, why should I?'

"Pastor says, 'I'll tell you why. I'll make it real simple for you, Ricky. What does Jesus Christ require of you? Did He forgive you?'

"'Yes, sir.'

"'Then you forgive your dad. End of story. How the Lord deals with your father is up to Him. But as for you, you do what He says. You got that?'

"I didn't say anything at first, so he started right back up. 'Don't you dare walk away, Ricky. Deal with your father. Give him to Jesus. Do right by the Lord. If you don't, I promise you, bitterness will follow you all your days. But if you do, you will break the cycle of violence that has dogged the men in your family.'

"I told him I want that—for me, for my girls, for my grandkids. I don't want what my dad did, or what I did, to be what they do.

"'Then pray,' he told me. 'Ask the Lord to help you give your father back to Him. Then stand back and watch Him answer that prayer. I tell you, there'll come a day when you will feel a new freedom inside you. You'll feel mercy for him. You'll know you've forgiven him. As long as you do it the right way.'

"'What way is that?' I asked him.

"'With all your heart,' he said. So that's what I'm doing. It hasn't happened yet. Probably won't till the nightmares stop."

"But your pastor's right," I said to encourage him.

"I know. And I really don't want to send the letter to Esther and Dora till it's over—till the Lord has given me peace between me and my dad."

I nodded and told him I understood.

He promised he'd send the last few pages of the letter when he finished it. I, in turn, promised to pray for him every day. For countless reasons, life got busy for both of us. We didn't see each other for nearly six weeks. We stayed in touch by phone or texting a couple of times a week.

Then one day I got a letter from him.

"It's time," he wrote. "I want to send the letter to the girls now. Read the end; tell me what you think." Attached were two handwritten pages. As I sat down to read them, I couldn't help but feel joy for Ricky. By God's mercy and kindness, he'd found a way to give his father back into the arms of his Savior.

That night, after he hit me, your grandmother spoke truth to me: "Don't let him change you, Ricky. That happened once. Don't let it happen again." It was hard. I didn't see him again till he was laid out in the church. I'm going to be honest. I was angry. I felt hate churning inside me like the old days—hate for what he did to me—hate for what he did to our family.

I went to my pastor. He told me the same thing your grandmother did.

When I began writing this letter, I had only one thing in mind. I wanted you to know the truth about what I did and what kind of man I am. The men in our family—dating back generations—have done wrong. Especially me. More than anything, I want it to end with me. I want to break the cycle of violence right here, right now, so your kids don't do what we've done. That's my prayer to God.

I'm not asking you to forgive me. I'm not asking you to love me.

But I am asking you to stand with me. Pray that the Lord sets our family free. Free from hatred and violence. Free from being one thing on the outside and another thing on the inside.

As for me, I choose to do what your grandmother told me to do. I'm clinging to Jesus. If He could forgive me for what I've done, then I choose to forgive my father for what he's done. I choose to be outside what I am inside and what I am inside to be what I am outside. And I pray to God, one day, when I'm stretched out in front of that church, you girls will say of your father, "He did it. He broke the cycle. And he did what we never thought he could do. He loved us—with all his heart."

    And I do.
    Daddy

QUESTIONS FOR REFLECTION

Consider mercy as an attribute of God's character. Talk about His desire for His mercy to shape and define your character and change how you do relationships.

Who do you need to give to Jesus? Is unforgiveness in your heart? Who is it you need to forgive as Jesus forgave you?

PART 3

THIS SON
OF MINE

16
SQUANDERING

~~*er*~~

Reflections on Luke 15:11–13

A man had two sons. The younger of them said to his father,
"Father, give me the share of the estate that falls to me."

—LUKE 15:11–12

Luke 15:1–2 tells us the Pharisees and scribes were grumbling at Jesus. They couldn't understand why He was a friend of sinners (see Matt. 11:19). Why receive them? Why eat with them? Didn't the law demand complete separation, no contact whatsoever? So why didn't He comply? In response, Jesus kindly told them story after story.

About His kingdom. About His Father.

At one point, He said that a man had two sons, wealthy sons. Rich in money, yes, but more: Their real riches had everything to do with the compassion that reigned in their home. These young men had what many in this world only dream of having—they were loved. They had their father's heart. What compares to that? These are the true riches God intends us to have, and these men had it in abundance.

It made them vastly rich.

But the younger son didn't see it that way. "Father, give me . . ." he demanded, wanting his share of the family estate. He wanted out. He wanted his inheritance. But could he really demand that?

Didn't that money only come after his father died, not before? Who does this? Why take what was not yet his? Wasn't he breaking the natural order of God's law? Didn't he know he was offending his father, treating him like he was already dead?

His father should have said no, but he didn't. He gave his son the money. He knew what no father should know—his son's heart had already gone cold. Soon enough, the young man gathered his things, loaded his transport, and left home. I wonder, as the son took off down the road, did he look back? Did he see his father's face?

Did he have any idea that, actually, he was the one who had died?

Why do these things happen? Why do our children break from us like that—taking what they can, despising our love, and choosing to live life contrary to everything they know is right and true? Outside their home, outside their God?

As his son disappeared over the horizon, perhaps part of Dad did die. No doubt, he had lost his son to a foreign country where he would worship foreign gods and squander his entire estate on parties and prostitutes.[1] He would squander it all because he had already squandered the one thing in life that mattered most: his dad's heart.

I imagine what happened next. His father marked the spot, the place where he last saw his son. And every day, morning and night, he would come back and stand there again. He would pray for his son. He would entrust him to almighty God and do what he couldn't stop doing—he would cry.

I called my wife on the drive home from work. "Hey, how was your day?"

"Did you hear about Callie?" Erilynne asked abruptly.

"No," I said. "What happened?"

"She's in the hospital. Dave called early this afternoon and asked if I'd go visit her. Of course, I said yes, so I did. I just got back a little while ago."

"It's not life threatening, is it?"

"I don't think so. I'll fill you in when you get here," she said, trying to be hopeful. But I heard a hesitation in her voice that concerned me.

As I pulled the car into the driveway, Erilynne stood in the yard with our old English sheepdog. She waved with a hint of a smile, but I saw the worry on her face. We've known Dave and Callie for the better part of ten years and Callie, especially, since she works side by side with Erilynne in the women's ministry at church. They're friends, talking every couple of days or so and sharing occasional lunches. Whatever this was, I knew it was serious.

As per usual, our sheepdog came running full blast the moment she saw my car. I opened the door and she came crashing in, barely letting me out. As I started playing with her, I kept my eyes on Erilynne, who was walking toward me.

"So, this doesn't sound good, huh?" I started.

"No," she said, shaking her head. "I'm not sure what to make of it."

"Why?"

"Dave asked me to call him when I got to the hospital. He said he'd meet me at the information desk and take me to Callie's room. I didn't think much of it, but it did seem a bit odd to me. Why didn't he just give me her room number?

Well, turns out, Dave wanted to talk to me before I saw Callie. He wanted me to tell me privately that she was admitted this afternoon to the psych ward."

"Psych ward? Callie?" I said, dismayed.

"Yeah, apparently she's been suffering from depression. He said the doctors think it's a hormonal imbalance. Apparently, she had a surprise pregnancy and miscarriage a few months ago none of us knew about. He said she'd handled it pretty well up to now. But I guess last night or this morning it got worse. He kept telling me, 'She's going to be fine. They just need to monitor her for a few days, that's all.'"

I could tell my wife wasn't convinced.

"When we got to the room, Callie's mom was there. She was friendly, as usual, and as adamant as Dave was— 'Everything's going to be fine. She's only in for a few days. It's been a rough time for her'—that kind of thing. But I could tell in Callie's eyes something else was going on."

"Like what?" I asked.

"Like fear. Like Dave and her mom are covering up what really happened. I mean both of them went out of their way to keep the conversation upbeat and pleasant. Callie was quiet for most of it. Then, a little while later when I started to leave, Callie grabbed my hand and asked me to pray for her—which I did—but after, she whispered, 'Can we talk?' I'm telling you, she's scared."

I tried to take it all in. It just didn't sound like Callie to me. "So if it's not only a hormonal imbalance," I asked, "what is it?"

Erilynne didn't hesitate. "I'm thinking the worst."

"Huh?"

"I think she may have tried to kill herself."

Just the thought shocked me. Over the next few days, I came alongside Dave as Erilynne continued to see Callie during visiting hours at the hospital. Callie was never alone. Dave or Erilynne's mother was always in the room with her. Erilynne couldn't shake the desperate look in Callie's eyes. A few nights later, Erilynne said she'd found something in one of her journals from a few years back.

"I want you to read this," she said, handing it to me. I took it, noting it was her prayer journal from 2010.

Sometimes I get the feeling I can't find the real Callie. She doesn't let me in. And when she does—when she drops her guard—I'm not sure I like what I see. Don't get me wrong. She's perfect for the women in our Bible study— especially the women she counsels. She's bright, gifted, attractive, and deeply respected.

Lord, I'm grateful for her. You know that.

Today, at lunch, I sensed it again. There were four of us at the table. We started talking about how You care for our most intimate, mundane needs. Jo shared, then Beckie, then me. Quite naturally, we turned to Callie. She was right there with us, engaged in the conversation, and quick to share a story—but not about her. For some reason, she deflected.

Maybe the others didn't notice. But I did. I never hear Callie's story. She never speaks about You in her life. She speaks about You in the Bible. She speaks about You in other people. *But never personally. Never about You and her together—from the heart, intimate and real. And I'm left wondering—does she know You? Is she with You? Or, in her heart, is she somewhere else?*

Is she, I wonder, like the prodigal son? I know she knows the power and depth of Your love for her. But does she believe it? Does she reject it? No, she's not living her rebellion out loud like the prodigal son. Nothing indecent. Nothing immoral. Just far away from You. That's how it feels to me. If this is true, Lord, help her. Bring her home. Please, don't let her squander Your love.

Please, in Jesus' name, bring her home.

QUESTIONS FOR REFLECTION

What does it mean to you that this young man squandered his father's love before he squandered his money? How much of this story is your story?

Have you ever gone to that far, distant country in your heart and soul—while keeping up your image to others? Are you doing that now?

NOTE

1. The expression "parties and prostitutes" is found in *The Living Bible* translation and resonates with how the older brother viewed his younger brother's escapades (see Luke 15:13).

17

PERFECT STORM

Reflections on Luke 15:14–16

*Now when he had spent everything, a severe famine
occurred in that country, and he began to be
impoverished . . . and no one was giving anything to him.*

—LUKE 15:14, 16

Curious, isn't it, how invincible we feel?

*We watch others slip and fall. Not us. We watch others lose
control and have to rely on friends and family to come to their
rescue. Not us; never us. We always have a plan, always a way
out—even if we don't know what it is. We're that sure.*

That invincible.

*The prodigal son spent everything. I wonder how long it took
him. Was it months? Years? Is it possible he didn't care it was
gone? Why should he? If he traveled in the right circles, if he
invested in people who had money, power, and influence and could
secure his future? Perhaps he fell in love with a wealthy young
woman. Or maybe his new business partners were swimming in
cash. Either way, surely he wasn't stupid. If his party life was to
continue, he needed to be wise, crafty.*

Especially now, with no money left. Did he feel invincible?

*The storm now raging around him was all his doing. He did
this—his decisions, his actions had left him bankrupt. But there
was another storm descending on him at the same time. A storm*

of greater power, mixing and converging with his own. This one was not his doing. This one came from God above. Bigger than him. Stronger than him. And not just for him—for everyone in the country. There came in those days a famine that hit and hit hard.

It devastated the nation. No food. Add to that, for him, no money.

Then came the test: Had he, in fact, invested in the right people? Would they see him through the storm? Surely they'd never abandon him, not then, not while people were suffering. Surely, they'd band together. He'd eat at their tables—like always. They'd weather the hard times with laughs, and he'd make it because he always made it. He came from privilege.

Maybe he still thought he was privileged.

But the doors shut. All of them. People who were his friends were not his friends. Not in the storm. He was left outside, impoverished and bereft. He did everything. He went everywhere. But "no one was giving anything to him."

He suffered hunger, something he'd never known before. What did he do? He had to do something. He had to eat. If he didn't eat, he'd die. So perhaps he walked the streets, pounded the doors, sun up to sundown, all day and the next, until someone gave him work, any work, just to feed himself. Just to survive.

And each day, perhaps he felt less invincible.

Finally, it happened. A job at minimal pay. He was sent to the fields—a hungry man charged with feeding hungry pigs. And there he was, watching them eat, wishing he could eat what they ate. Who does that? Who dreams of eating as pigs eat?

As the perfect storm raged on.

"Hey," Erilynne said. It was a little past two when she arrived at Callie's hospital room. She was surprised to see her alone.

"Perfect timing," Callie smiled.

"Nobody here today?"

"Mom's here. She just went down to the cafeteria to get some coffee and make a few calls."

Erilynne hugged Callie and sat in the chair by her bed. For the first time in a week, Callie looked more like herself. She had color in her cheeks and a quiet softness in her eyes. The pale, harried look was gone. After a few minutes of catching up, Callie reached for Erilynne's hand.

"Before Mom comes back, I've got to tell you some things."

Erilynne leaned in and took her hand.

"A few years ago, I started having panic attacks. Dave was having a hard time at work. He'd come home, wound up and angry and dump it on me—which was fine. I want him to do that. But add the stress of two kids at two different schools, keeping up with the house, working with you at church, and out of nowhere I start getting these panic attacks. So I called my doctor, who sent me to another doctor, and eventually I got on antianxiety meds."

"Did Dave know?" Erilynne asked.

"I didn't tell anyone. Dave had too much on his plate. Plus, I think it would've freaked him out if he knew I'd gone to a psychiatrist for meds. I handled it on my own, and it worked. For the most part, the panic attacks stopped.

The meds gave me that little oomph to keep me balanced. It was no big deal until, well . . ."

Callie paused, dropping her eyes.

"We weren't planning on another baby. Dave was actually happy about it, so, naturally, I tried to be too. But honestly, I didn't want it. I could barely handle two, and the idea of having a newborn in the house sent me over the edge. The panic attacks flared. So I called my doctor to see if I could increase the dose, but she told me not during pregnancy."

"You mean, she took you off the meds completely?" Erilynne replied.

"You got it."

"So what did you do?"

"I managed. What else could I do?" She let her words hang in the air a little too long. Seeing the concern in Erilynne's face, Callie quickly explained, "Oh, no, I'd never hurt this child. You've got to believe me. I didn't do anything to cause the miscarriage."

Erilynne squeezed her hand and assured her, "I believe you."

"It just happened. At about eleven weeks, I started bleeding. We went to the hospital, but there was nothing they could do. Dave was totally upset. He kept trying to comfort me, promising me we'd have another. I didn't have the heart to tell him I didn't want another. I didn't want this one."

Callie's eyes filled with tears.

"I went back on the meds as soon as I could. I tried to get my life back to normal, but I felt so guilty, like I'd done something wrong by not wanting the child. And somehow, I felt responsible, like I caused the child to die. Stupid, huh?" Callie reached for Kleenex. "So, I started upping the meds on my own."

Callie wiped her eyes and stayed quiet for a minute. "I guess I took too many," she confessed. By the look on Callie's face, Erilynne couldn't discern whether she'd done it accidently or intentionally. As gently as she could, Erilynne pressed in and asked, "Callie, did you mean to?"

"You have to promise me something," Callie said abruptly, avoiding the question. "You can't tell anyone I've been in the psych ward. I don't want anyone at church to know. Promise me." She was adamant. "I don't want people getting the wrong impression of me."

"Callie, I promise. That's between you and Dave."

Then came the real push from Callie. "Promise me I can stay in the women's ministry. All of it—the Bible teaching, counseling, decision making. I don't want this to change anything. Not between us. Not in the ministry. Nothing, OK?"

Callie had that desperate look back in her eyes again—like she could feel her world coming apart. As if this one act of hers, this stupid act that landed her in the psych ward of a hospital, could make everything come crashing down around her. And somehow, she figured Erilynne was the one person who could make sure her Humpty-Dumpty life was safe and pieced together again.

Later that night, at home, all Erilynne could say to me was, "It was really sad."

"What did you say to her?"

"Nothing. Her mom walked in and ended the conversation. Callie kept looking at me with those big blue eyes of hers, wanting some confirmation that I'd make this promise too. But I didn't give it to her. Before I left, I told her we'd talk again soon. What else could I do? Her life is way out of control, and it's not my job to rescue her. That belongs to Jesus."

"But you said she never talks about Him."

"Not a whisper."

QUESTIONS FOR REFLECTION

Have you ever felt invincible? Have there been storms in your life bigger than you? What was your low point—your "pigsty" experience—like?

On hitting bottom, did you try to fix things yourself? Or did you turn to Christ and rely on Him?

18

UNCOMMON SENSE

Reflections on Luke 15:17–19

But when he came to his senses, he said, "How many
of my father's hired men have more than enough bread,
but I am dying here with hunger!"

—LUKE 15:17

How long did he stay with the pigs?

Why does it take so long for common sense to kick back in—
especially after we've trashed it, beaten it down, and mocked its
stupid reminders so we could go and do what we never should
have gone and done? When it does kick in, why does it take us
so long to listen to it? To listen and act? To act so we can
change?

At some point, the prodigal son remembered his father's
hired men.

No doubt he used to work with them every day in the fields,
side by side. Some of them he may have known from childhood.
Perhaps, some he even grew up with and played with as friends.
And maybe, now, they too work in the fields. All of them hired
servants but really, more like family.

They had it better than he did now. Their stomachs full. Their
beds warm. Their bodies and clothes clean—all because their
boss provided for them and loved them. His boss didn't. His boss
never would. Why was he still here?

Common sense: Go back home. Get a job with your father.

How long had it been since he'd thought about his dad? Or remembered the look on his face when he grabbed the money and took off? He didn't care about him then. He cared now, only because he was hungry. He'd die here if he didn't do something. He needed to go home. It was common sense: Make things right.

But things weren't right. He knew that. Yes, it was what he did to his parents. But more, it was his life here, the choices he'd made, the fun, parties, women, laughs—all of it. If he went back, was he ready to say what needed to be said?

"My father, I have sinned . . ."

The words must have been bitter in his mouth. But it awakened another sense—an uncommon sense—long since gone and buried. It took him back to his childhood, back to when he knew God and what God required of him. He knew right from wrong. He knew God loved him. And he knew now—he'd turned his back on Him.

That uncommon sense: Get right with God.

Why? Because he'd sinned against Him too. He chose the selfish life, the immoral life. Dishonoring his father and mother. Breaking every law God had ever set up for his good. He had to say it again, but this time with his eyes to heaven.

"My Father, I have sinned . . ."

Why does it take so long for us to hear this uncommon sense? And when we do, to act on it? This time, the prodigal did. He left the pigs behind. He grabbed his few remaining things and began the long journey home. It was time to start putting things right.

"I am not worthy to be your son . . . Make me like your hired men—fed, clothed, warm, and alive."

Even now, I imagine, the bitter taste remained. After all he'd done, why should his father—why should his heavenly Father— even give him audience? He wasn't worthy of it. He didn't deserve it. And for the first time, maybe ever, he knew it.

It was the last time Erilynne saw Callie at the hospital. She was discharged the next day and, soon enough, Erilynne knew she'd be calling—pushing—to resume her position at church. But how was she supposed to respond?

In her prayer journal, she wrote the following:

I am terribly confused. Again, I say, Callie is good at what she does. She appears strong and confident in her relationship with You. This is what makes her a good Bible teacher. It's why women seek her out for counsel and prayer.

So why can't I hear the sound of You in her? It's like she knows You for others but doesn't know You for herself.

Years ago, at a dinner party, Callie's mother made the strangest comment to me: "She'll hide in the shadows if you let her. Always living somebody else's story. Not her own." At the time, I didn't think much of it. But it stayed with me. And now, I wonder, is this the real Callie? Not the gifted Christian leader but the one hiding in shadows? I feel like this is the one I met at the hospital.

And now, she's scared. She needs me to pretend I never saw her like that, so she can go on being what everyone needs her to be.

Two very different people.

Father, I don't know what to say to her. Help me help her. Give me wisdom. Scatter the shadows around her

*and bring the light of Your Son into her heart. I pray
this through Jesus Christ my Lord. Amen.*

Erilynne texted me at work Wednesday morning: **Guess
who's coming to see me this afternoon.**

Callie? I texted back.

**She wants answers. She's back at the women's Bible
study tomorrow.**

What are you going to say?

Don't know. Grasping at straws. Pray for me.

A little later that afternoon, Erilynne sent me an e-mail.

Thad,

*Callie arrived a little past one. Relaxed and easy-
going. We sat in the kitchen. I made some iced tea, and
we chatted for a while. Mostly about what she's been
doing since she left the hospital ten days ago: Dave, the
kids, getting back into routine. She's still a bit overwhelmed by all the cards, flowers, and meals that came.
She said she never expected it in a million years.*

"You are very loved," I assured her.

*She gave a quick nod and admitted, "I'm nervous
about tomorrow."*

"Are you ready to come back?"

*"Yeah, I think I am," she said, but the push was gone.
And then she told me that was why she'd come. "But is
it OK," she asked "just to be there and not do anything?"*

I couldn't hide my surprise.

"I need some time off," she said. "I know this is going to sound crazy to you. But I'm going to say it and hope you understand. I'm wrestling with something. I'm wrestling with whether I'm a Christian or not—I mean, really." And then she looked at me, waiting for a reaction, wondering if she should go on.

"It's OK," I whispered.

Then she said, "You know, it wasn't my first time in the psych ward. Yes, as a patient, it was, but I've been there as a counselor to other women. So when I was there, I decided to counsel myself. What I said to them, I said to myself: Do this. Pray this. Read this. Try this. All common-sense principles from the Bible. It may have helped others . . ." She shook her head, looked straight at me, and winced. "I actually laughed out loud," she said.

"Why?"

She didn't respond at first. She sipped her tea. She tried changing the subject. It was odd, but again I saw her as a prodigal daughter: stuck at the pigsty, having no idea how to get home. She rambled a bit but eventually circled back.

"I have a hard time receiving," she shared. "When I'm the center of attention, I never feel worthy of anybody's love—let alone God's. And now, after what I've done, I don't know what to do. I mean, I've got answers for everybody but me." And then she pointed to her heart and quietly said, "It's not here."

I felt at that moment like Callie was actually stepping out of the shadows. Somehow that sense inside us— that call to be right with God—had somehow awakened in her. And now, I could see in her eyes the question I'd been hoping she'd ask: She wants a relationship with Him.

Not wanting to presume, I asked, "Can I help?"

"Would you mind?"

I told her I'd love to. And somehow, in that moment, it felt like the prodigal daughter wanted me to help her come home. Amazing, huh?

Erilynne

QUESTIONS FOR REFLECTION

Think about times you've come to your senses. How long did it take to listen, act, and change? How about with your uncommon sense?

Both the prodigal and Callie are taking action steps to get right with God. What do you need to do? How do you help others do the same?

19
COMPASSION'S KISS

Reflections on Luke 15:20–21

So he got up and came to his father. But while he was
still a long way off, his father saw him and felt compassion
for him, and ran and embraced him and kissed him.

—LUKE 15:20

I wonder what he looked like at that point.

Was the son wearing the same work clothes—dirty, torn, and smelling of pigs? When did he last bathe? Cut his hair? Get a good night's sleep? The long journey from that distant, once-Edenesque country must have taken its toll. When did he last eat? Was his face lean, his body skin and bones? Was he sure he'd make it home?

One bare foot in front of the other.

I wonder if he found mercy along the way. It's hard to find safety on roads notoriously filled with thieves and villains. Did he care? Did he travel alone? Were there others with him? Surely it wasn't like before when he had transport, money, weapons, and bravado. All of it gone. How long did it take? Weeks? Months?

And what did it feel like to step back into the land of promise?

Did he experience even a glimmer of joy? Or was there fear—fear someone might know him? What if someone called him by his real name: "the man who spat in his father's face"? And what would people say when he got to his hometown? Would they remember him? Would they despise him? Would they even recognize him?

He had been cocky then.

Perhaps he kept his head down as he walked. Maybe he rehearsed his lines: "I've sinned. I am no longer worthy. Make me your servant." But would that work? Was he even worthy to be his father's servant? What made him think his father would have anything to do with him? Should he turn back? But where would he go? He had no place. It's possible his world felt small, wrapped in a dark, depressive cloud where questions haunted him: "If this doesn't work, why live? Why go on?"

Still he took steps.

And finally, one day, it happened.

He lifted his head and saw the miraculous—the altogether unexpected. His father was coming. He was running at full stride with servants running alongside. His father's arms were open, his face filled with joy, his voice crying out for him, and running like he wasn't going to stop—like soon their bodies would collide.

And maybe that's what happened. The force of his father's body hit his and up he went—lifted into the air. His thin, almost weightless body in the clutches of his dad with kisses, and laugher, and shouts of joy that maybe, yes maybe, made him break into a shriek of joy too.

Such love! Such mercy! Such kindness! Embraced in his father's embrace and kissed so hard it almost hurt.

Dave had done his work well. The news had spread quietly through the church that he and Callie had lost a baby, she was recovering well, but it was a harder road back to health than expected. So the moment Callie stepped back into church that Thursday morning, well-wishers swamped her.

"It couldn't have gone better," she told Erilynne, taking a seat next to her after the Bible study was over.

"Do you think people understand your need for time off?"

"I do," Callie said, "for now. A couple of women asked me when I was coming back. I told them I wasn't sure."

"You OK with that?"

"Yeah. I mean, part of me wants to jump back in now. Just being here today made me realize how much I love these women. I love praying with them, counseling them—definitely my sweet spot. And plus, it's what Dave wants."

"Dave?" Erilynne asked, unsure.

"I think he'll feel better when everything's back to normal. But I'm not ready," Callie said definitively. "That was also pretty clear today."

"Really, how?"

"There's a woman who's been coming the past few months. You probably don't know her. She gets here late, sits in the back, and leaves before it's over. I'm not sure how she got my name, but I saw her a few times before I went into the hospital. The last few weeks, she's called nearly every other day—I think genuinely concerned for me. But she really wants to meet again."

Callie's face looked both compassionate and annoyed. "But I get it; I really do," she went on. "She's had a terrible life. Abused by her dad and, worse, she looks just like him. So does her second-born son. It's like everywhere she turns she sees him. She's constantly fighting depression, suicidal thoughts, alcohol addiction, everything. I'm just glad she's coming to Bible study."

"Sounds like a big step for her," Erilynne commented. "How'd she react when you told her you weren't ready?"

"She was pretty upset. I anticipated it, though. A few days ago, I called Mary Anne and asked if she'd be willing to see her, to pray with her, and she was. I think Mary Anne's a perfect fit. So I presented that option to her."

"That go over well?"

"Not really. But it helped clarify something for me. I'm not ready, not yet. And I'm afraid"—Callie paused— "really afraid—that I might never be. How can I give her what I don't have? She's begging me to show her how to receive Jesus Christ into the most intimate places in her life, her deepest, most profound hurts. She doesn't want platitudes. She needs real, practical help."

Callie got that desperate look in her eyes again. "If I had the guts, I'd tell her the truth, that I have no idea how to do that. She needs more than I can give her. All these women do. They deserve more."

Erilynne listened, but didn't say anything at first. It's always been hard with Callie. She's a trained counselor. She's brilliant—so brilliant that she easily uses the skills of her mind to deflect the issues of her heart. Because of it, she sets up huge, impenetrable walls. Walls that need to come down and come down now. But how? Why is it so hard for her? It's the simplest of all things.

So simple a child could show her.

"A few years ago," Erilynne said, "I remember you gave a Bible study to the women here on the story of the prodigal son. Remember that?"

Callie nodded.

"I listened to the recording again recently. It was really well done. You let us see the father's heart and how his compassion, his kindness toward his son is a picture of God's compassion for us. You showed us the joy, the delight, of what it means to give compassion. What if we changed the conversation?"

Erilynne couldn't read Callie's expression.

"What if, instead, you and I talked about the joy of *receiving* His compassion?"

Still Callie didn't move.

"Think about that young man. He's coming home, feeling unworthy. He has no right to expect anything from his father. And yet, all of a sudden, he looks up and sees him running toward him. Running with all his heart. His arms open wide. As the young man stands there, he's suddenly in his father's embrace. He's being loved. It's that simple. It's what we do with our children. And all they do is receive it. We pick them up and love them, embrace and kiss them, all because they belong to us. It's the same story here.

"Callie, you and I belong to our Father. We're His daughters. All He wants is for you to come home, open your arms, and let Him embrace you with kisses."

Tears came. She didn't bother to brush them away. Almost reflexively, she picked up her purse and stood. One last time, she looked at Erilynne. Her eyes sad, filled with inexpressible pain.

"I just can't," she said. And with that, she turned and was gone.

QUESTIONS FOR REFLECTION

When have you ever felt unworthy—dirty, torn, and smelling of pigs? What's it like to see your Father running toward you with mercy and love?

Why, when we feel worthless, is it hard to receive His compassion? What blocks us? How can we learn the childlike pose of opening our arms to Him?

20

ADORNED

~~~

Reflections on Luke 15:21–22

*And the son said to him, "Father, I have sinned against heaven
and in your sight; I am no longer worthy to be called your son."
But the father said to his slaves, "Quickly bring out the best robe
and put it on him, and put a ring on his hand and sandals on his feet."*

—LUKE 15:21–22

He wrapped himself around his son's neck like a warm blanket
in winter and refused to let go. I try to imagine his joy and the
roar of praise to God that bellowed deep from within his soul.
Finally, God had answered his prayers and brought his son home.
Kisses—a thousand and more kisses.

He wasn't dead! All those years he feared he was dead. But
he wasn't. He was alive and warm and whole and—beyond
imagining—here in his arms!

"Father," the young man said.

Perhaps their eyes met. Really met. Oh yes, his face had
changed. So much about him had changed. But at the same
time, nothing had changed. The eyes were the same eyes the
father saw when he first held him as a baby. The nose, the mouth,
the color of his hair, the voice—this was him, the son he'd lost,
standing here, found.

"I have sinned against God."

No doubt his father was still breathing hard from the run.
Maybe he stepped back but didn't let go. He listened, but it took

time to hear because it was everything—absolutely everything—that he was feasting his eyes on his son! Did it matter, really matter, if his son had come back still wild in his rebellion? Yes, but no, but still he'd have run just as hard. Just as fast. Just to hold him again—he was alive! Not dead.

"I have sinned against you."

Could his father hear the longing in his voice? It was different from before. Back then, his son was defiant. But look at him now! Was he hearing what he thought he was hearing? These words from his son, these first words, weren't about money. He wasn't asking for help with his physical needs. He was trying to get right with God. Right with him. It was about matters of the heart. He wanted to be family again.

"I am no longer worthy to be called your son."

But this time, did he really hear the boy? Did he, and not understand it? Did he, and reject such a thought? Did he, and did it move his heart to the very depths that his son had suffered even to the point where he felt he was no longer worthy to be his son?

The young man had more to say. He'd rehearsed it before: "Father, make me as one of your hired men."

But by that time, it didn't matter. His father's voice was already issuing the command for his servants to quickly adorn his son in the finest robes. Then, ensuring family status, he ordered they bring the family ring. And with it, soft sandals for his son's callused, bloodied feet.

In this act, he was declaring the best news of all: This son was his son indeed.

I wonder, just then, did he run back into his son's arms again—clothing him with his love, adorning him with a fierce tenderness that had been pent up all those days, all those months, all those years?

Late that same afternoon, Callie texted Erilynne: **I'm sorry for running out. It was a little too much. Forgive me?**

Erilynne responded, **Yes, but I'm sorry too. I shouldn't have pushed—forgive me?**

Yes, but it's what I need. Can we meet soon?

They texted back and forth until they found a time. Erilynne added, **Mind if I send an e-mail tomorrow?**

I'd love it! Callie wrote back.

This, Erilynne knew, was a safe way to communicate with Callie. One-on-one could sometimes be hard for her. Especially when the conversation became too intimate, too personal. It was better this way. She could write and give Callie space and time to wrestle with it. But, she wondered, how far should she go?

Callie—

A few years ago, I wrote in my journal that you remind me of the prodigal son. Not that you lived like him, but that you saw yourself like him: unworthy, undeserving.

I can't imagine what it was like for him to stand there—his self-value still back with the pigs, the mud, the slop, his body still aching with hunger—and feel his father's love, his embrace, and his zeal to welcome him home. How does anybody do this? Just open our arms to receive what we don't deserve?

It's easier to say, "May I be a farm hand?"

In other words, "Let me serve. And help. But don't make me what I'm not. Don't force me into your arms and make me feel the strength of your compassion for me. I am no son. If you knew the real me—the pigsty me—you'd never do this. So, no, don't love me. Let me love you by serving you and let's leave it at that."

You see, that way, this young man's self-image can stay with the pigs. He doesn't have to open his heart to his father. Instead, he can convince himself he's doing the right and noble thing. He's taking a position of humility by being nothing more than an out-of-sight, no-name farmhand. He can stay in his self-pity while, at the plantation, his family feasts around the dining room table.

Why? Because he convinces himself he is, always is, unworthy of their love.

But here's the ironic twist: When we think this way, what we think is humility is actually a deep-seated arrogance. We take a position that suits us, not our Father. This isn't what He wants. It's what we want. By refusing His love, we reject His love. We reject Him. We can't do this. You see, our Father loves us. He wants us to believe in His love, not run from it. I know this sounds too simple, but let me say it anyway: "Callie, open your heart and receive." But I know, I really do know, it's not simple. We spend a lifetime forging our identity. We know the real us. Can we really dismiss it all, just like that? I ask it again: How do we do this? How do we receive what we know we don't deserve?

But that's the story.

Callie, you're not a farmhand in the kingdom of God. You're His daughter. You've been bought by the precious blood of His Son. He wants nothing more than to clothe you in all the robes of daughtership. Say yes. If it's hard, really hard, then ask Him to help you. Pray the prayer deep in your soul, "Lord, help me to believe."

And then, open your arms. Open your heart. And wait for Him. Soon enough, He will come, and the words of the prophet will suddenly burst into life over you:

> *The LORD your God is with you,*
> *the Mighty Warrior who saves.*
> *He will take great delight in you,*
> *in his love he will no longer rebuke you,*
> *but will rejoice over you with singing.*
> *—Zephaniah 3:17 NIV*

You have my love,
Erilynne

A day passed, then another. Callie didn't e-mail back. Or text. Or call. Nor was she in church the next Sunday.

An hour before she and Erilynne were supposed to meet, Callie sent a text: **Sorry, can't come. Not ready.** Surprisingly, she didn't come to the Thursday morning women's Bible study that week. Or the next.

It was three weeks before Erilynne saw her again. Every month, on the fourth Friday night, there's a prayer meeting at one of the inner city churches. It's a night filled with worship and praise. Young and old; black, white, and Latino; inner city and suburban; this denomination and that—all come together to worship Jesus Christ and pray for the city's welfare. It's a night where the pastors help people experience a deep, intimate sense of the Lord's presence.

Callie would never come to a night like this. It was simply "too experiential," she'd say. But this night was particularly engaging. Pastors spoke on the need for each of us to be "strengthened with power through His Spirit in the inner man, so that Christ may dwell in your hearts through faith . . . and to know the love of Christ which surpasses knowledge" (Eph. 3:16–17, 19). People were turning to each other and praying for each other to experience the power of this love.

And surprise!

Erilynne whispered in my ear, "Across the aisle, three rows back." I looked and saw Dave and Callie. There were people surrounding them, praying for them, laying hands on them. And there they both were, eyes closed, faces bathed in tears, and their hands gently lifted in surrender.

QUESTIONS FOR REFLECTION

Why were the prodigal's first words about his relationship with God and his dad? Aren't we usually more concerned about our physical needs?

How do you receive what you know you don't deserve? How do you open your heart and receive real mercy?

21

A WONDERFUL TIME

Reflections on Luke 15:23–24

*"Get a grain-fed heifer and roast it. We're going to feast!
We're going to have a wonderful time! My son is here—given
up for dead and now alive! Given up for lost and now
found!" And they began to have a wonderful time.*

—LUKE 15:23–24 MSG

It all happened so fast.

*Next thing he knew, he was being swept along to the main
house. I imagine his father simply couldn't contain his joy. He
commanded his servants prepare the kitchen and take the best
from the flock. Perhaps some were sent to tell his wife and family,
while others took the news out to their neighbors, inviting them
all to the feast. It was time to clean and decorate the homestead
for celebration.*

*"Tell them all," he said, "my son is here—given up for dead
and now alive!"*

*I wonder if his father ever let go of him. Was the young man
ready for all this? Ready to face his family? Face all his friends
and neighbors? To have this huge party and be the center of
attention? What was this moment like for him?*

One step and then another. Each one, no doubt, a choice.

*And what was it like to come home? Who came out to greet
him? His mom, his grandparents, the household slaves? No, not
his older brother, but what about his brother's wife and children?*

Were there other siblings? Were there cries of joy? Was he engulfed in their embrace? How did it feel to be welcomed, wanted, and loved?

One step and then another.

I imagine him being taken to his childhood room with servants attending. Perhaps they brought him food, real food and not pig food. And perhaps they helped him get ready for the feast—one cutting his hair; another treating his sore feet; while another drew a bath so he could be clean again.

No doubt downstairs was a buzz of activity. I wonder if, looking out his bedroom window, he could see the heifer being prepared and the servants smiling and happy. Everything smelled like home. Everything in its place, like he'd never left. Like what happened never happened. But it had. He knew it. He knew everybody coming knew it. What would they think of him? Would they say, "How can you wear your father's robe after what you've done?" And what would he say in response? How could he face them?

How could he deal with his own sense of shame?

Soon enough, the house would fill with people. They'd see his father's joy and enter into it with music and laughter, food and the smells of a feast like no other. All he had to do was put one foot in front of the other, descend the stairs, and jump into a sea of people. Each step, a choice—a real choice to receive it all.

And he did—or, at least, he made a start.

Clearly, everybody was having "a wonderful time." This can only mean they'd welcomed him. They saw him as his father saw him. They, too, made a choice to celebrate his return. Perhaps he heard "You've made your father so happy!" or "We never stopped praying this day would come!"

One step at a time.

Earlier that morning, he'd had one prayer: His father would hire him as one of his servants. And now here he was, dressed in his father's robe. Wearing his father's ring. He had to accept it somehow. The very same love he once rejected he had to learn to receive. This feast was a first step. The road would be long. He knew that. It would take time to be part of the family again. But, for now, I imagine one thing rang true in his heart. He was starting to feel clean again—on the outside, yes, but on the inside too.

Mid-Saturday morning, Callie texted Erilynne: **I know you don't look at e-mails on the weekend. Make an exception?**

Erilynne wrote back: **Love to. Out doing errands. Will call or text later.**

She couldn't help smiling. This had to be good news from Callie.

Hey—

Surprised to see me last night? Me too.

I have so much to tell you. Let me start by saying that your letter was spot on. I have no idea how to be His daughter. Farmhand, yes. Self-worth back at the pigsty? Absolutely, for as long as I can remember. But see Him running for me? Feel Him clothe me in robes of daughtership? Watch Him call for a huge celebration and make me "worthy" to sit at His table? It terrifies me—all of it.

I'd rather eat with the servants.

So, I made a choice. I started praying like you said: "Lord, help me to believe." I asked Him to show me how to open my heart and receive His love for me. I told Him I was scared. I told Him I didn't know how to do it or where to start. And a few days later, I think He answered that prayer. I knew exactly what to do.

I had to tell Dave—everything.

So I did. One night, late, we talked. I told him about the panic attacks, the meds, what it was like coming off them during pregnancy, the guilt of not wanting the baby, and then my blaming myself for the miscarriage. It made him uncomfortable. But I wanted him to hear the whole story. I told him I didn't try to hurt myself. It's just that I couldn't handle the guilt. I wanted the ache in my soul to stop. It's why I took too many pills.

At some point, he stopped listening. He didn't want to hear it.

But I kept going. I went back to my childhood, my low self-image, all the studying I did in college to compensate. Then after we married and had kids, it's like we built this image together we had to keep up for our family and friends. I told him I couldn't do it anymore.

"You'll be fine," he said coldly.

Image is everything for Dave. I know that. But I need him now. I need him to walk into this story with me and help me rebuild my life. I asked him if I could resign from my counseling practice at church, but it freaked him out. He got angry and told me not to do anything. We'd sleep on it and talk in the morning.

We didn't.

The next Sunday, he said he wasn't feeling well enough to go to church. The next weekend, we were out of town. He made excuses for missing his regular church meetings and Bible study. I knew well enough to leave him alone. Eventually I circled back and told him we needed to talk. He didn't want to. So I did what I thought was best. I told him I wouldn't resign. I'd start back up in a few weeks.

He didn't say anything, but I could tell it's what he wanted.

So, a few days ago, I decided to go to the Friday night prayer meeting in the city and told him. He seemed fine with it but last night, as I got ready to go, he was upset with me and told me it wasn't safe for me to go alone.

"Then come with me," I said. "I'll get a sitter for the kids."

He hemmed and hawed but finally agreed to it— reluctantly. It was a big step for him, and I was glad for it. Well, that is, until the service started. The first half hour was way beyond our comfort zone. Both of us wanted to leave. But at some point, I realized, this was it. This was everything you had talked about. I needed to open my heart and receive what the Lord had for me.

Sounds selfish, but I stopped worrying about Dave. I opened my hands, quietly confessed my sin in repentance, and asked Jesus to come heal me. I did what I could to surrender myself to Him. Next thing I knew, people were praying over me, and I was crying. I felt, really felt, His embrace—as a daughter.

Without any sense of shame.

I know the journey ahead will be long. Each step, a choice. But I want it more than ever. Somehow Dave must have known that. I have no idea what he thought of last night, not yet, he hasn't told me. But this morning, out of nowhere, he said he's fine with my resigning. If I want to, I can. Then he took me in his arms and told me he'd support me. No matter what it takes. Or how long it takes.

Can you believe that? So here I go, one step at a time, thankful you're here with me.

Callie

QUESTIONS FOR REFLECTION

How did the young man face all the people at the party? Have you ever wrestled with shame? What kind of choices need to be made at times like this?

To receive God's mercy is to be changed by it. Can you take the steps Callie is taking? Do you ever feel the resistance Dave feels?

22

OUTSIDE AND COLD

Reflections on Luke 15:25–32

"Your brother has come, and your father has killed the fattened
calf because he has received him back safe and sound."
But he became angry and was not willing to go in; and
his father came out and began pleading with him.

—LUKE 15:27–28

It must have seemed unreal to the prodigal son.

With the stroke of his father's wand, he was the prince at the ball. More like a hero than a godless, immoral son. Is it possible every conversation went well—with no awkwardness whatsoever? No reference to the indiscretions of his past? Perhaps not here, not now, not inside his father's house. Perhaps, on this special occasion, everybody fell under his dad's spell. A gracious night, filled with joy.

Until the news came.

His older brother was out there. And he wasn't happy.

He'd been working in the fields all day. The crowd inside, the sound of music, had confused the older son. When he asked about it, he was told everything and exploded in anger at his father. He didn't understand why he'd welcomed "this son of yours" back, let alone killed the best of the herd. After what he'd done? After years of wild living? The older brother's soul raged. Of all people, who deserves the party? Who's the faithful son?

It was just the two of them outside. Father and older brother.

For the young prince, the magic spell must have vanished into thin air. He knew, better than anyone, that only a few short hours ago, he was dressed in filthy rags—hungry, smelly, a beggar for his father's mercy. So why was he now dressed in a Joseph-like family robe? Was this the real him? Or was the real him that other man—clothed in filthy rags, having wasted his family's money on pleasure and prostitutes?

His brother would never forget. The stench would never go away.

At some point, his father came back in the house—alone. The young prince would soon learn his father's pleading had not worked. His brother was still out there, his heart angry, bitter, and cold. It hadn't gone well. The older son had said things no son should ever say to his father. And yet, his father persisted. He begged his son to come inside and celebrate the best, most wonderful news: God had answered his deepest cry!

"My son was dead and now he lives! My son was lost and now is found!"

With that, the story abruptly ends with no resolution. We know the young prince is safe inside the home—received back into the family. But his older brother is still outside and cold in heart. What happened to him? Did he ever reconcile with his father? Did he ever come back into the embrace of his family? Is it possible he left home that day—for good?

We don't know. But what we do know is the father's heart. If his oldest son did leave, no doubt come first light of dawn the next morning, he'd do what he'd been doing for years. He'd go back to the same place. He'd follow the same pattern of his devotions. He'd cry out for his son, his other son, and he wouldn't stop, not until his prayers to God were answered. Morning and night—for as long as he had breath.

A few days later, Callie made her decision.

"Well, she did it!" Erilynne told me. "Callie read her resignation letter at the women's Bible study. She was brilliant!" Erilynne handed me the letter. I was struck by her honesty and humility. I read part of it out loud.

We always want to put a good face on, don't we? I do, anyway! It's hard to admit when we're not doing well. Or we need something. Or we're lost and can't seem to find our way. We don't want people to think less of us. But sometimes, I think that's the best place to be. Jesus said, "Blessed are the poor in spirit."

It's where I've been these past months. And as hard as this is to say, I know for me to be the woman the Lord wants me to be, I need to step away from what I do for Him and learn to receive from Him. I've lost that in my life, and I'd like you to help me find it. And though I resign my position today, I'm not going anywhere. I'll be here at church and on Thursdays like always. But I need your prayers. This is a big step for me and a scary step.

"It's beautiful," I said.

"I agree, and so did everybody else. They just love her."

"What about Dave? How's he doing?"

"She says he's very supportive."

"I'm concerned about him. Something's not right."

Erilynne looked at me, surprised. "I'll speak to her," she said, and she did. Over the next few weeks, they spent more time together than usual. Callie was far more relaxed as she talked freely about her new relationship with Jesus.

"It's like what I know in my head," she confided to Erilynne, "is slowly seeping into my heart. But sometimes it feels like a rollercoaster ride. Sometimes, I feel the nearness of the Lord's presence in my life, but other times, I just don't know. I start doubting. It's like I'm Cinderella. One minute, dancing at the ball and the next, I'm back in my dirty old rags, feeling that sense of shame again."

But each time they met, Callie seemed a little bit stronger and Erilynne made sure to always ask about Dave.

Her response was the same, "He's great!"

But eventually, Erilynne pressed in. "It's just that we're not seeing him as much. It seems like he's pulled back from nearly everything at church."

"He's busy at work, that's all," Callie explained.

But that changed the morning Callie called in a panic. "It's my fault," she told Erilynne. "I'm pushing him away."

"What happened?"

"Last night, we were talking like we always do. I want him to know what's going on with me. So I told him what the Lord is doing in my life—the really good things and the really not-so-good things. But the second I started, he lost it. He said he's done with all this—he doesn't want to hear it."

The line went silent as if Callie was trying to collect herself.

"It got worse. He said he's done with church. He's done with our friends from church. He wants no part of it. Then he said he's not even sure about us. He's confused. He doesn't know who we are as a couple anymore. All he wants is for things to be the way they were. He wants the old Callie back. He doesn't like the new me—always talking about Jesus. He's done, I mean, really done."

"Oh Callie, I'm so sorry," Erilynne said gently.

"I don't know what to do. I'm losing him."

"Just be patient," Erilynne assured her. "It happens sometimes."

"What do you mean?"

"The Lord is in the business of changing us, isn't He? And sometimes that change causes friction in our marriage. Change isn't always easy. And, if we're not careful, we might push our spouse away."

Callie took a deep breath and asked, "So what do I do?"

"Let's start with what you're not supposed to do. Don't stop pursuing the Lord. But at the same time, don't patronize your husband. Don't judge him. Don't talk about him to other women in a condescending way. So many women do that, and it's wrong. Instead, ask God to give you wisdom.

"Just remember the Lord was kind to you. Like the prodigal's father, He waited and watched for you. The moment He saw you, He came running with open arms. Do the same with Dave. Wait for him. Pray for him. Love, be patient, and be kind to him just as the Lord has been patient and kind to you. You just need to slow down a bit with him, that's all."

"I'm so scared," she said. "What if he's done with me? What if it's already over? What if he comes home tonight, packs up, and leaves me and the kids? What then?" Just the thought made her cry. "I can't lose him. I don't want to lose him." And then, she did what was so hard for her to do in the hospital. She turned to Jesus and asked Him for help. She cried and prayed and begged Him for Dave.

"Lord Jesus, bring Dave close to you. Don't let his heart grow cold."

A simple prayer to the One she now knew holds her tight in His embrace.

QUESTIONS FOR REFLECTION

On what grounds is the anger of the older brother justified? Why is it hard for those who feel they've earned God's favor to be with those who've freely received His mercy?

When have you experienced this friction with those you love? When one is changing in Jesus and the other wants no part of it? How do you handle it?

PART 4

THE ROYAL FAMILY

23

NAOMI

Reflections on Matthew 1:5–6 and Ruth 1:1–18

*Salmon was the father of Boaz by Rahab, Boaz was
the father of Obed by Ruth, and Obed the father of
Jesse. Jesse was the father of David the king.*

—MATTHEW 1:5–6

*The gospel news is the best news: Mercy himself was born
in Bethlehem. Mercy died for us on the cross and when we
receive Him, we are changed by Him, and mercy begins to shape
our character. He makes us a people of mercy.*

*This has always been God's plan. We see it in the genealogy
of our Lord listed in Matthew 1. Look at them, men and women
of mercy—like Boaz and Ruth.*

*And Naomi. At first sight, as we read the story, we might get
the wrong impression of Naomi. She's poor, troubled, and bitter.
The storyteller reveals nothing of her early years. There's no
record of her childhood days—her father, mother, or siblings. We
know nothing of the joys they shared or the trials they suffered.
But one thing we know: They must have known God and His
mercy. Why? Because here in Naomi's darkest days—it's there,
inside her, strong and undiminished.*

For this is God's story with God's people.

*Back in ancient time, God entered into a legal, binding
covenant with Abraham and his offspring. In the terms of that*

covenant, He promised mercy and lovingkindness (in Hebrew, chesedh) would stand between them forever. Of all words, this one reveals the heart of God. It speaks of His goodness, mercy, faithfulness, and incomprehensible, inexhaustible love.[1]

He promises it. He gives it. We are shaped by it.

The storyteller doesn't tell us how chesedh formed and fashioned Naomi's soul—just that it did. We see her in her most troubled days. She and her family were exiled to the land of Moab due to a famine. While there, her husband died. Then, after ten plus years in Moab with her two sons and their wives, death came again and took both her sons, leaving her childless and alone.

She had every right, in her grief, to cling to her daughters-in-law. But she did not. It's here where we begin to see God's chesedh in her. She chose their welfare over her own.

We see it on the day she began her long journey back to Bethlehem. She spoke to the young women, urging them to stay in Moab and find husbands who would give them rest. She wanted what was best for them—not her.

They mattered first.

And what do we see? This same chesedh is etched on Orpah's and Ruth's hearts, too. No doubt, they had learned the mercy of the God of Israel from years spent under Naomi's care. Naomi now sees it in them. Before she sends them back to their family homes, she praises God for the chesedh they've shown: "May the LORD deal kindly [chesedh] with you as you have dealt [kindly (chesedh)] with the dead and with me" (Ruth 1:8). It was there, inside them. There in Orpah as she remained in Moab.

And there in Ruth. This chesedh captured Ruth's heart. She knew this chesedh of God stood between her and her mother-in-law, Naomi. And she spoke it out loud. She would not leave her. Nothing but death, she vowed, would ever break them apart.

And there they were—just the two of them—on the road to Bethlehem. Poor, bereft, yet having the one thing in life that mattered most: They were bound to God and to each other in this chesedh *mercy of God.*

"You holding out on me?" I asked Pastor Adams. He didn't flinch. I didn't expect him to. It was a cold Saturday afternoon in late January. We were in the church basement at the kitchen counter getting some coffee. The wide open space behind us was filled with round tables and folding chairs.

There were about fifty of us that day.

For as long as I can remember, Adams has run a food pantry out of his church on Saturday afternoons. It's the one place Christians from all over the city and suburbs can come together week after week to serve people in need.

"What are you talking about?" he belted out, not even looking at me.

"I found this card in the bathroom," I said as I held it up. On it were two stick figures—one washing the feet of another. In big, bold caps were the words THE NAOMI PROJECT and, at the bottom, in simple script:

Building the Character of God's Mercy in the Christian Soul
Eight O'clock—Second Wednesdays

"Louis!" he called out as he stirred his coffee. Pastor Adams, a football player in his day, six foot four, at least two hundred seventy-five pounds, has a commanding voice. As we walked to a nearby table, Louis appeared. Adams pointed to a seat and said, "He wants to know about the Naomi Project."

Louis sat down, looked at me, and said, "Changed my life." It surprised me. I'd known Louis for a while now and never heard him mention it before. "About ten years ago, I started coming here 'cause of Charlotte. We were seeing each other. I told her I wanted to move in with her, but she said no. She told me she was saving herself for the man God had for her."

He leaned in and quieted his voice.

"That didn't work for me. So one night, when I had too much to drink, I forced the issue. Again, she said no. One thing led to another and I hit her. She ran out, telling me she was done with me. Next thing I knew, Saturday morning comes and a whole bunch of people from church are working in my front yard. I come out and say, 'What do you think you're doing?'

"Old man Freddie was around in those days. He's with the Lord now, but I'm telling you—no one messed with Freddie. Not because he was a big man—he wasn't—but because he got in your face like a bulldog. Am I right, Pastor?"

"Uh-huh," Adams grunted, giving a half smile.

"Freddie tells me, 'Charlotte belongs to us. And we're coming back here till you do right by her.' Then he gives me that card in your hand and says, 'If you want to make something of yourself, Louis, it all begins here.'

"Man, I was so embarrassed! Everybody in my yard knew I'd hit Charlotte—and still they came, witnessing the love of Christ to me." He leaned back in his chair as if he'd finished the story and said, "Rest is history."

"So what's the Naomi Project?" I asked, intrigued.

"Pastor calls it a 'training center,'" Louis said. "He only lets people come who mean business with God. You've got to want to follow Jesus and make a change in your life or you're out. He tells us what's killing our community is how we treat each other. There are too many men cheating on their wives, too many kids neglected, too many teens with time on their hands, too many of our elderly abused and forgotten. He says if we restore honor in our families, we restore honor in our community. And if it doesn't start with God's people—"

"It won't start at all," Adams said, finishing his sentence, "because that's what the Bible says. It's the kindness of God that leads to repentance. And kindness isn't something we talk about, it's something we do. Just like God did when He sent His Son to Bethlehem and then to the cross— that's the kindness of God! And when you have it, you have Him. And when you have Him—"[2]

"You do what He does," Louis continued. "And that's the Naomi Project. We're learning to be kind as God is kind in our families and in our community."

Just then, a little girl, maybe three years old, came up to Louis. She was adorable, dressed in tiny blue jeans and a pink T-shirt with the words, "I'm a Naomi girl!" written over her heart. She squeaked, "Daddy!"

"This is my baby girl," he said playfully, picking her up. He looked over at Pastor Adams and said, "And I know, better than anyone, I'd never have her in my life if you all didn't come that Saturday morning and bring the kindness of Jesus Christ into my life. You gave me a chance. You gave me Charlotte back."

"The Lord did that for you, Louis; you know that," Adams teased.

"What are you saying? The Lord came to clean my yard?"

"You got that right!" Adams laughed out loud. "Looking just like Freddie!"

QUESTIONS FOR REFLECTION

How has this mercy, this *chesedh* of God, impacted you in the past? How is He making you a person of His mercy in the present?

What if our churches had something like a Naomi Project? How would we affect our communities if "kindness isn't something we talk about—it's something we do"?

NOTES

1. The Hebrew word *chesedh* is best translated "lovingkindness" or "mercy." It is the foundation of God's character (see Ex. 34:6–7). It is the promise given to us in covenant (see Ps. 103:4, 8, 11, 17) and the essence of how we are to conduct ourselves with others (see Mic. 6:8).

2. Some of Scripture's most powerful verses relate this truth: Romans 2:4; Titus 3:4–5; and 1 Peter 2:3.

24

UNPROTECTED

Reflections on Ruth 1:19—2:3

*And Naomi said to Ruth "It is good, my daughter,
that you go out with his young women, lest in
another field you be assaulted."*

—RUTH 2:22 ESV

They arrived in Bethlehem.

But where would they go? Where would they stay? Was there family nearby to feed and care for them, to provide shelter and protection? It's not like they slipped into town unnoticed. People were talking. The city was stirred (see Ruth 1:19). They were saying, "Is this Naomi?" They heard about her husband and sons. About Ruth the Moabite. And about Naomi's new name: Bitter.

Maybe for a night, or a week, they had provision and protection.

But it was the busy season of harvest. And at some point, it seems it was just the two of them again, alone. Maybe relatives gave them a place to stay and a few spare clothes to wear. But poor, widowed, childless, and hungry, they needed something to eat—now, today, in order to live. Something had to be done.

Perhaps Ruth thought begging was the only option. But Naomi knew God, who gave Israel laws for situations like this.

That's all Ruth needed to know. She asked her mother-in-law for permission to go into the fields to get food—and to pray for favor (see 2:2). She needed someone to treat her kindly.

Naomi didn't go with her. Why? Was she sick? Had the journey from Moab sapped her strength completely? Were her emotions too raw—everyone seeing her like this? Maybe she wanted to go for Ruth's sake. It's not clear why, but she doesn't go with her and she allows Ruth to go alone, early in the morning, no doubt hungry.

They needed food today.

Morning came. People were heading to the fields for work. The sun began to bathe the land in light and drive the dark away. But there was another kind of dark out there—lurking, threatening, dangerous, and Naomi knew it.

Did Ruth? She must have . . .

In those days, in that culture, like it or not, women came under the protection of their husbands, fathers, or male relatives. Bearing their name made them untouchable and safe. Without that covering, there was risk—terrifying risk. Especially for the single, young, and beautiful. But even more so for a Moabite, a foreigner. Ruth did not belong to the daughters of Israel. Of all women, she was most vulnerable.

Still, she went out.

At great risk. She must have known she had no honor, no worth in this culture—and that she was vulnerable prey to young men who would possibly assault her. And yet, still, she went. It was her choice to be kind now. She must care for Naomi more than herself. Her mother-in-law needed food. She needed food.

Each step, a risk. Each step, a choice.

It must have been hard for Naomi to let Ruth go that morning. Harder still to pray. How could she pray when it felt like the Almighty had turned His back on her and afflicted her? Would He hear her now? In her bitterness and pain? Would He be kind and merciful to her daughter-in-law Ruth? Would He give the favorless any favor at all?

As Ruth slipped out the door, unprotected.

I hurried in the side door of the church, drenched from a downpour of rain, and heard the sound of little children everywhere. Toddlers mostly. As I hung my raincoat on a nearby peg and started down the hall, peering into the classrooms, I realized I had no idea Pastor Adams's church had a preschool, a nursery for infants, and a program for older children with special needs.

As I passed one of the rooms, I thought I glimpsed Pastor Adams off in the corner. I stopped and backtracked a few steps. There he was, sitting in a chair too small for him, holding a crying young boy in his arms. When he saw me, he held up his hand and pointed toward his office. I nodded my head and went to wait for him there.

This was my doing.

I'd asked to meet him. I wanted to know everything about the Naomi Project. I even asked if I could attend the Wednesday night monthly meeting. He said, bluntly, "Not yet." But he did agree to see me. I found his office, sat in one of the chairs in front of his desk, and waited.

"You always on time?" he thundered when he walked in a few minutes late. Like always, I got a bear hug and a slap on my back that made it sting.

"Pretty much," I replied.

"Not a bad trait," he jabbed, as he moved toward the big leather chair behind his desk. He went right to task. "We started the Naomi Project twenty years ago."

"Why Naomi?" I asked quickly.

"Because life was hard for her," he said slowly, rhythmically. "Everything she had was taken from her. But even then, she chose a better way. Even when it felt like God wasn't on her side, she put her daughters in the school of God's mercy and kindness and taught them that no matter what life brings, no matter what life costs us, we do for others. We always do for others."

He looked at me like I should know these things.

"Why do you always talk about mercy and kindness?" I continued.

"Because it's who God is," he shot back quickly. "Think about it. When King David entered into covenant with Jonathan, they promised 'kindness' to each other. When Jonathan died in battle, David asked, 'Who in his family can I be kind to?' [see 2 Sam. 9:1–3]. And guess what he did? King David took Jonathan's crippled son and made him his own. You know this, right?"

I nodded, but I hadn't really thought of it like that.

"That's what happens to us in Jesus. He took us into His family and promised us kindness. One day in glory we're going to know 'the surpassing riches of His grace in kindness toward us in Christ Jesus' [Eph. 2:7]. But for now, He calls us to live it. He puts us in Naomi's school of kindness so we can learn it. So we can do it right here on the streets of our community. How else will people come to know Jesus?"

"So what does that school look like?" I started to ask. But a boy was standing behind me, sniffling. The same one Adams was holding when I first got there.

"Come here, son," Adams said, his voice quieter. The boy, maybe eight years old and with a slight limp, came around the desk and folded into Adams's embrace.

"This is Hernando. Three years ago, we found him sitting outside the convenience store down the street crying and scared, with bruises on his face, like someone tossed him out of a car and just left him there to die. He belonged to nobody."

The boy turned to look me, his eyes moist and sad.

"Even to this day," Adams said, "we don't know who his people are."

The boy, rubbing his knee, said, "Papa, make it go away." Pastor Adams put his hand over the boy's and whispered a prayer in his ear. He leaned back in his chair, closed his eyes, and gently rocked.

"There, there, it's gonna be all right now," he said tenderly.

A minute later, Adams went on with his story. "Next meeting of the Naomi Project I told the people of God we needed a family to step up. Every child deserves a home. No one goes unprotected or unloved. Somebody needed to show mercy and kindness today. Not just for a little while. Someone needed to open their heart and take Hernando into their home as their own."

Hernando opened his eyes and frowned.

"One of the elders began to pray for Jesus to open hearts for Hernando. As we prayed for this little boy, I looked over and saw my wife bent over in tears and I shook my head, saying, 'No, Lord. You know we can't do this now.' "

I sat there quietly, trying to take it all in.

"Two of our kids were already grown. Our youngest was a year away from graduating high school. My wife and I were dreaming of the day when we'd be empty nesters and have some time to ourselves. But the Lord had other plans for us, and I needed to open my heart to Jesus. Isn't that right, son?"

The boy giggled the cutest giggle ever.

"It's better now, Papa," he said. "Better now."

QUESTIONS FOR REFLECTION

What do you think it was like for Ruth to go into the fields unprotected? Have you ever cared for someone else at great risk to yourself?

Consider the cost of *chesedh* to Pastor Adams and his wife. Do we open our hearts like this? Why don't all our churches have Naomi Projects that focus on extending sacrificial mercy to those in need?

25

YOU SEE ME?

Reflections on Ruth 2:3–10

*How does this happen that you should pick me out
and treat me so kindly—me, a foreigner?*

—Ruth 2:10 msg

I wonder why nobody gave Naomi counsel, saying, "Don't send Ruth to the fields on the east side of town. It's dangerous for her there. But send her over by—" Had it been too long for Naomi to remember these things from her past? We don't know. We only know she allowed Ruth to go out that morning with no sense of where was safe, who was safe, and who was not.

And off Ruth went, following the workers into the fields.

She knew protocol. She found a field to work in and went to someone in charge and said, in accordance with the law of Moses, "Please let me glean" (Ruth 2:7). She told him she was a foreigner and she belonged to Naomi. That should have been enough.

And it was.

The first morning passed without incident. I wonder what it was like for her. Did anyone talk to her? Was she welcomed? Was she pushed aside? Was there talk, banter, unkind things said about Moabites? Or was it the opposite? Was it like she was invisible, unseeable? And what about the young men? Did they stay at a safe distance?

It seems she worked hard that first morning.

Near midday, the owner came to the fields and the miraculous happened. He saw her. He asked about her. And then he went to her.

"My daughter," she heard. Somehow she knew who he was. But how? Perhaps the workers around her whispered, "The master is coming!" But why talk to her? Was there any room in her mind for the slightest possibility that he could see her, the invisible?

I wonder, did she stand to greet him? Or did she stay bent over, as if frozen in fear, as she heard him speak gently to her, "Listen carefully, my daughter." And then came the unthinkable. The man offered her kindness beyond imagining. He spoke in the language of mercy.

"Do not glean in another field, nor leave this one. Stay with my maids. Let your eyes be on these fields where they reap and go after them. Have I not charged my young men not to touch you? And when you're thirsty, go, drink to the full!" (Ruth 2:8–9, paraphrase).

How was this poor Moabite woman able to bear the weight of his mercy? We are told she fell with her face to the ground. Did she wonder why he was doing this? Why was he caring for her, protecting her?

From somewhere inside her, quite unexpected, courage rose to speak. "You give me favor," she said to him. "But I'm a stranger. I'm a Moabite. Yet, you see me."[1]

When I met with Pastor Adams, I asked for two things: (1) to attend the monthly meeting; and, (2) to interview people from the Naomi Project. He handed me a workbook and DVD and said he'd think about it.

I took that as a yes.

Two days later, I sat at my office desk, put the DVD in my laptop, and realized I had my first request. Last month's meeting had been filmed. Splashed across the screen, in big letters, I saw:

THE NAOMI PROJECT
Changing Attitudes, Building Character,
Impacting Our World for Christ

I quickly learned the format for the night: (1) worship and Bible teaching; (2) prayer in groups of three or four; and (3) reports from the past month, testimonies of answered prayer, a listing of the most pressing needs facing the local community, and a discussion on how to meet those needs.

The church sanctuary looked full of people. In my journal, I wrote a short excerpt from Pastor Adam's Bible teaching. I loved the way the congregation chanted their response:

PASTOR: From Psalm 136, we learn God is good.
PEOPLE: His lovingkindness is everlasting.
PASTOR: And when He created the heavens and the earth, how did He do it?
PEOPLE: His lovingkindness is everlasting.
PASTOR: When He stretched out His strong arm to redeem the children of Israel from the bondage of slavery, do you know why He did it?
PEOPLE: His lovingkindness is everlasting.

PASTOR: Verse 23 says He remembers us in our low estate. Psalm 107:1–2 says the redeemed of the Lord know why He rescues us in our times of trouble.

PEOPLE: His lovingkindness is everlasting.

PASTOR: So tell me why He came to Bethlehem. Tell me why He went to the cross. And tell me why He came to you when you cried out for help.

PEOPLE: His lovingkindness is everlasting.

PASTOR: So how can we hear the cry of others, sit back, and do nothing? Are we not to treat them with the same kindness as He treated us? So I ask you, are we doing what He did for us with our elderly? Our spouses? Our kids? Those in our families? Our friends? Our brothers and sisters in Christ? And what about the people suffering in our community tonight? Right here on our streets? If we can hear their cry, what will we do?

PEOPLE: His lovingkindness is everlasting.

At that moment, the congregation stood to their feet and applauded. When they sat back down, Pastor Adams spoke for a while longer until he asked everyone to break into smaller groups to talk and pray over his message.

The DVD was not edited.

For the better part of thirty minutes, the place erupted in conversation and prayer. I forwarded the video until a man rose to the microphone and called the place to order.

"I'm Brother Johnson," he began.

"Last time we met, we told you a fourteen-year-old girl named Angel went missing down near the corner of Main and Maple. That's all we had. We told you to fight for her in prayer. We figured she'd been trafficked. Three families from the Naomi Project made Angel their focus this past month."

Two men and a woman came up alongside Johnson.

"We found her house, but nobody was there," one of the men reported. "We soon learned Angel's mother was staying upstate with her brother. We drove up to see her, but she was too drugged out and didn't know about Angel."

"We then took to the streets," the other man said. "Drug houses, pimps, people who might know where she was. We also talked to the police. Then, ten days ago, we found her being held in a juvenille detention center here in the city."

The second people heard she'd been found, the place broke into applause.

"We got permission to go see her," he went on, but the woman next to him moved toward the microphone.

"We learned that Angel was trafficked," she said. "But God rescued her. The police busted the house where she was staying for drugs. The men who took her were thrown in prison and they put Angel in juvie. Last weekend, sister Laqueta and I went to see her, and I want you to hear what we found."

Laqueta came up and stood next to her.

"Oh, she was skin and bones something terrible," Laqueta lamented. "She couldn't even look us in the eyes, poor girl. She must've thought we'd come to hurt her somehow. But all we did was love on her."

"That's right," Pastor Adams said from behind.

"And we told her God loved her and, from now on, things were going to change for her—and change for the better. She has a new family now who love her. She has a new family who's going to pray for her and stand with her through thick and thin. She's a Naomi girl now, we told her. Yes she is!"

Again the place broke into applause.

"'Course she didn't know what that meant!" Laqueta smiled. "But we promised her a safe home where nobody would ever hurt her again. And I'm telling you, it was the saddest thing I've ever seen. Angel looked right up at us with tear-filled eyes and said with a small, beaten-down voice, 'You don't mean *me*, do you?'

"We told her, 'We sure do mean you!'

"'You care?' she said, shaking her head. 'But nobody cares about me. Nobody even knows I'm here.'"

QUESTIONS FOR REFLECTION

Consider Boaz seeing Ruth. Why is it so hard for those high up to see the lowly? What kind of eyes does it take for us to have Boaz's eyes?

How can we who have been rescued by Jesus hear the cry of others, sit back, and do nothing? And how can we hear their cry if we're not intentionally listening?

NOTE

1. Robert L. Hubbard, in his commentary—*The Book of Ruth* (Grand Rapids, MI: Eerdmans, 1988), 165—notes the Hebrew expression is "you have noticed the unnoticed" or "recognized the unrecognized."

26
UNDER COVER

~~~

Reflections on Ruth 2:11–18

*May the LORD reward your work, and your wages
be full from the LORD, the God of Israel, under
whose wings you have come to seek refuge.*

—RUTH 2:12

Upon reading this text, it's clear that Boaz chose not to see
Ruth's outward appearance—her old clothes, the dirt on her
hands, or the sweat on her Moabite face. Nor could he see her
youth or beauty or even the obvious signs of prolonged hunger
that likely marked her physical frame. He chose to see honor.

You see, Boaz knew her story. He knew she'd left her parents
and her country. She chose, instead of remaining, to love her
mother-in-law to the fullest, sacrificing even her own happiness.
After burying her husband, she chose to come to a people she
didn't know and tuck herself safely under the wings of the
Almighty.

Choosing then, choosing now, the way of kindness.[1]

This, Boaz knew, is the mark of God on the soul. For the God
of chesedh makes His people a people of chesedh. And this, he
knew, was Ruth. All that she had done had been fully reported
to him and, because of it, he spoke words of blessing. "May
the Lord reward you," he told her, "and make you whole and
complete!"[2]

But it confused Ruth. She knew she was nobody. So why did he lower himself to regard her? Why extend favor? Why speak comfort and kindness to her? "My lord," she said, "I'm not like one of your maidservants."

He wanted to do more for her.

At mealtime, he went to her again. He invited her to eat the midday meal. It must have taken her breath away. He sat her at the head table—with the reapers—and, no doubt, near to where he himself sat, the highest place of all. How was she supposed sit there and be seen in front of everybody?

And then—more. She is given a plate of food piled high. More food than she could ever eat. And who would serve her? Who'd do that? Who'd bend that low and serve the lowest of all the owner's servants?

It's him, she discovers. It's the owner himself who "served her roasted grain" (2:14).[3]

And she ate. She ate until she felt what she hadn't felt in so long—satisfied. And when she was done, she was told she could take the leftovers home with her—a cooked meal for later.

Then off she went, back into the fields. The afternoon wasn't like the morning. Boaz had instructed his reapers to treat Ruth with special favor. And they did, throwing stalks of barley down in front of her. By day's end, as she beat out what she'd gleaned, she had more grain than a week or two of common labor.[4]

Did she run home happy? Was Naomi standing at the door, waiting? Could she see the joy in Ruth's tired face and know her prayers were answered? Ruth was safe! Ruth was unharmed! Her arms were full of harvest and blessing.

And something more.

There in Ruth's hand was the most precious gift of all. The one Naomi needed and needed now. Not the raw uncooked barley. But the cooked grain—the leftovers from lunch. She must have taken it quickly. She must have been hungry beyond words.

And as she ate, she must have known—didn't she?—God wasn't against her after all.

He was for her. He was gently, kindly, lifting up her head.

A few days later, Pastor Adams called and left a message: "If you still want to interview somebody from the Naomi Project, call Laqueta." He left her phone number. I assumed it was the same woman on the DVD who'd gone to see Angel in juvie. I was thrilled to have my first interview and called her.

"Nelson here," a man answered.

"I'm calling for Laqueta," I began.

"She's not here right now. Is this Pastor Barnum?"

"Yes, how'd you know?"

"Pastor Adams said you'd be calling. And we'd be happy to meet with you. We were thinking tomorrow, 4:15, at 365 Maple Street?" I told him I'd make it work and thanked him. His name wasn't familiar and, the next day, when I got to the house and saw him sitting on the front steps, I knew we hadn't met before.

"Laqueta's inside," he said, after we talked a while. I soon learned it was Angel's mom's house. With her mom back in town, Angel spent time with her after school though she didn't live with her anymore.

"Angel stays with us now," Nelson told me. "Her mom can't take care of her. Don't know for how long, but her mother doesn't have a good track record getting off drugs. We've got another family at church helping her."

"From the Naomi Project?"

"Yeah, she needs a lot of care. She's got to let the Lord do what she can't do for herself. But in the meantime, we keep Angel safe."

"So, how'd you become part of the Naomi Project?" I asked.

"It was Blake," he said. "I'm hoping you're about to meet him."

"Who's he?"

"To be honest, somebody I've hated all my life. We were teenagers on the street." He pointed to a scar over his left eye. "Got a concussion from this one. We've always had it out for each other. Few years back, I gave my life to Christ and did my best to stay away from Blake. He was a bad influence.

"Then, eighteen months ago, he had a car wreck—totaled it. No idea how he survived. That's when it started for me. I tried praying for him, and I couldn't do it. I went to Pastor Adams; he heard me out and told me I needed to go to the Naomi Project meetings. My wife, Laqueta, was already going."

"Did it help?" I asked.

"Yeah, I needed an attitude change. Eventually, I asked God to help me pray for Blake. Then, six months ago, it happens again. He gets in another car wreck and nearly dies from it. So I start praying for him. But this time, God says, 'Go!'"

"Go?"

"I suddenly realize I'm supposed to do more than pray for him. I'm supposed to get down to that hospital and *show* him the love of Christ. And that's exactly what I did. I tell him, 'I don't want you dying without Jesus. Two times you've had car wrecks. Are you sure you're ready to face God?'

"He blows me off, saying, 'What do you care?'

"I say, 'I do care, and I'll prove it to you.' From then on, I started doing what Pastor Adams taught me to do. I started showing him kindness—in the small things. In the big things. I haven't stopped to this day. Even now, though I know he hates it. He wants nothing to do with Christ or with me. At least, not yet."

I look at him, confused. "So why's he coming here?"

"Because two days ago, I learned something about him. So, I go to his house last night. He tried to push me away but I say, 'Not this time, Blake. You're going to want to hear what I got to say. There's business between us now.'

"'What business?' he says, getting right in my face.

"I say, 'It's time you do right by your daughter.'

"He pushes me back and says, 'What I do, what I don't do, has nothing to do with you.' I tell him I'm not fighting him anymore. Not since Jesus came into my life. He knows that about me now. That's when I land the news on him. I tell him, 'I know you don't have custody of your little girl.'

"He says, 'So?'

"I say, 'You know her mama's not doing well. Till she gets back on her feet, she's got Laqueta and me taking care of your daughter. You got that? Angel's with us now—under my roof. Under my protection. You want to see her, you want to be the dad God wants you to be, the kind of dad she needs, then you be at her mama's house tomorrow at 4:30.' And I left."

"What did he say?" I asked, wide-eyed.

"Nothing. He turned around and slammed the door. But, for me, I couldn't let him find out any other way. It had to come from me. If he won't be there for Angel—then he needs to know I'm doing what he's not doing."

Then I heard it: a car door closed. I turned and saw a man coming toward us, peaceful and calm. Nelson stood up quickly but said nothing.

The man also said nothing, but said everything with one quick motion of his hand. He raised it up and met Nelson's in mid-air with the sound of a clap.

Like they were old friends.

QUESTIONS FOR REFLECTION

What do you think it was like for Ruth to receive the abundance of blessing from Boaz? Why is it hard for us, the undeserving, to receive the same from our Lord (see Eph. 1:3–8)?

When have you found mercy to be persistent, annoying, and a challenge to your soul? Consider Isaiah 66:2 and apply it to yourself.

NOTES

1. In Ruth 3:10, Boaz described all that Ruth did for Naomi (described in 2:11) as "kindness," or *chesedh*.

2. Robert L. Hubbard, *The Book of Ruth* (Grand Rapids, MI: Eerdmans, 1988), 165.

3. Ibid., 175. Hubbard wrote, "Indeed, *he* served *her*!" How perfectly this portrays our Lord who came not to be served, "but to serve, and to give His life a ransom for many" (Mark 10:45). See also, Luke 12:37; John 13:5; and Philippians 2:5–11.

4. Ibid., 179. Hubbard argues the normal take for a worker in that day was about "1–2 pounds per day." An ephah "weighed about 29 (US) pounds," which means Ruth brought home "the equivalent of at least half a month's wages in one day."

27

HEAR MY PRAYER

~~~

Reflections on Ruth 2:19—3:9

He said, "Who are you?" And she answered, "I am Ruth, your servant. Spread your wings over your servant, for you are a redeemer."

—RUTH 3:9 ESV

Boaz didn't tell her everything—why? Midmorning, she'd asked him straight out, "Why have I found favor in your eyes?" Boaz could have told her then what the reader already knows. And yet, he didn't.[1]

Why not say, "Ruth, we are family"?

But this isn't why he showered her with favor and kindness. No, not because she was family, but because, in his eyes, she was a woman worthy of honor. He made this quite clear to her earlier in the day when he said to her, "All that you've done for your mother-in-law . . . has been fully reported to me. . . . May the LORD reward your work" (Ruth 2:11–12).

As Ruth went home that first night, she still didn't know.

It was Naomi who told her. When Ruth spoke Boaz's name, Naomi burst into a song of praise to God: "May he be blessed of the Lord who has not withdrawn his kindness [chesedh] to the living and the dead." Naomi quickly told Ruth, "This man is our relative."

The women were safe now. Boaz had promised Ruth protection and provision for as long as Ruth chose to stay in his fields. And

Ruth did—gleaning every day, week after week, for the two months of the barley and wheat harvest. We don't know if she continued to sit near him every mealtime, whether there were more conversations between them, or whether the reapers were as generous to her as before. If so, Ruth and Naomi would have enough food for an entire year.[2]

But there was another miracle—beyond all the others.

The second Naomi heard the name of Boaz she recognized it and told Ruth: This man, according to God's law and the customs of the time, is "one of our closest relatives." That is, he had the right, the power, to be their "redeemer."

Was the concept foreign to Ruth? At some point, Naomi must have explained all of it to her. If Ruth was willing, there were customs to be followed. She'd need to know what to do, how to do it, and when to do it. And for Ruth, the decision came quickly.

"All that you say I will do."

She followed Naomi's instructions. She washed, anointed herself with perfume, donned the best of her dresses, and snuck out into the night, the dangerous night, alone. She made her way to the threshing floor and, like her mother said, Boaz was there. She saw Boaz, but he didn't see her. No one saw her as she hid in the dark. She waited until he finished eating. Then longer, as he found a quiet place to sleep.

At just the right time, she went to him.

According to custom, all she had to do was uncover his feet and stay there. This small act would tell him why she was there and what she wanted. She did it; yet he didn't stir. As the night passed, he suddenly awoke and sat up, knowing someone was there but not knowing in the dark who. He said quietly, "Who are you?"

"I am Ruth your maid," she replied. Perhaps she held his uncovered feet in her hands. But lest the night's sleep rob him of understanding, she said, perhaps in a whisper back, "Spread your covering over your maid." Words that could easily be translated *from deep within her soul: "Come, my redeemer, and be the answer to my prayer."*

"Nelson, I should go," I said, soon after he introduced me to Blake. He nodded slightly, and I knew I'd guessed right. He needed time with Blake and Blake needed time to get reacquainted with his daughter.

"Call me sometime," Nelson said, and I told him I would.

As I made my way to the car, I noticed two women passing by the house. They looked familiar, but I didn't know why. As I got to my car, I saw Eddie across the street talking on his cell phone. I knew him from Pastor Adams's Saturday afternoon food pantry. When he saw me, he waved.

I crossed the street, shook hands, and waited for him to get off the phone. "Hey, how you doing?" he said when he was done. We talked for a while before I asked, "So what's going on? What brings you here, Eddie?"

"Same as you," he replied, pointing to Angel's house across the street.

"You're here to see Angel?"

"No," he said emphatically. "We're here to pray." When he said "we" he pointed down the street to the two women I'd just seen walk by the house. Eddie told me the one on the left was Alberta, the other, Gracie. "Can't do this work without prayer. You know that, right?"

"Yeah."

"And you just saw a big answer to prayer. Can you believe Blake showed up?" he said as he put his phone in his back pocket. "Few years ago, I went to Pastor Adams and told him I was troubled by something. I asked him, 'Are we just a bunch of do-gooders?' You see it on the news all the time—people doing good for people. So, I asked him, 'What makes us different?'

"Pastor said, 'Say what's on your mind, Eddie.'

"So I told him. 'Never send a team out unless you send the military with them. You can't do kindness and mercy like God does kindness and mercy without the power that comes through prayer. We need the secret forces sent out to do battle. If you want the Devil's hands off our community, send out the military!'

"Pastor Adams just stood there looking at me. He said, 'What's got you so fired up about this anyway?'

"I said, 'What if I told you it was my mama?'

"I'm telling you—that made him smile! I told him, like I tell you, when I was twenty-five I was no different than Blake. Nobody got in my way. I ran the drug scene. I did jail time. I was out for me. Till one day, I was laying on my living room floor, drugged out. No idea I was at death's door. I opened my eyes and saw my mother standing over me, praying out loud.

"'Lord, don't take my boy now,' she said. 'You can have him when He knows You. I'll give him to You myself. But Jesus, Lord Jesus, not now. Don't take my boy now. I ask You to save his soul first. Deliver him from drugs. Free him from the Devil's power. Heal my boy. Lord, hear my prayer and rescue him.'"

Eddie shook his head. Just the memory stole his breath.

"That prayer changed my life," he finally said. "From that day on, I never looked back. The resurrection power of Jesus Christ came into my life. And you know when Pastor Adams heard that, he said, 'We're never going to be a bunch of do-gooders, Eddie. If the Holy Spirit isn't in charge, if what we do isn't done in prayer, we're not doing it. From now on, you're heading up the military.'

"I told him I would, and that's why we're here today."

From behind me, Alberta and Gracie came up alongside. "Did you see that?" Alberta said. Eddie and I looked over at the house. Nelson and Laqueta were standing at the front door. Blake was sitting on the steps in front of them. Next to him was his daughter Angel, his arm gently wrapped around her.

"That right there," Eddie declared, "is the power of God answering prayer!"

"Come on, Eddie," Gracie said. "We're not done here."

"No we're not," he said, and the three of them started walking down the street. Eddie turned and asked me to join them. As I did, I heard Gracie ask the Lord to protect Angel's heart, rescue her mother from drug addiction, and save her father's soul for the kingdom of God.

"Cover them, Lord," Alberta urged, "and spread Your wings over this family. Be their Savior and Redeemer."

Eddie, song-like and a little too loud, said, "Amen. Lord, hear our prayer."

"Shhh," Gracie said, poking him.

And on we walked. A secret military force quietly pushing back the powers of darkness so that each act of kindness, each ounce of mercy, might bring the light of Jesus Christ into the people of this community for His name's sake.

QUESTIONS FOR REFLECTION

Up to now, we see mercy caring for Naomi and Ruth's immediate needs. How does mercy go deeper with their need for a "redeemer"? How is it the same for us?

What is the relationship between mercy and prayer? Do you have as fierce a commitment to prayer in your life as Eddie did? At your church? If not, what could strengthen that commitment?

NOTES

1. In brilliant storytelling, the reader learns that Boaz was family at the start of Ruth 2. Ruth learned his name on her first day gleaning but didn't find out he was actually family until Naomi told her in 2:20.

2. Robert L. Hubbard, *The Book of Ruth* (Grand Rapids, MI: Eerdmans, 1988), 191.

28

BEST THERE IS

———✎———

Reflections on Ruth 3:10—4:6

*Now, my daughter, do not fear. I will do for you
whatever you ask, for all my people in the city know
that you are a woman of excellence.*

—RUTH 3:11

She knelt there at his feet, in the middle of the night. She was
asking him to do what God, in His law, required him to do. Yet, that
responsibility was not first his. It belonged to another member of
their family, he told her, but still, Ruth had surprised him.

"My daughter, do not fear," he said.

The law given by God through Moses states that when a man
dies without an heir, the closest relative must—at great financial
cost—perform the duty of family. He buys the man's land. He
takes his widow and, through her, produces a child who will never
be his. Not really. For the child will bear the name of the woman's
dead husband, the child's "father." And when the heir is old
enough, he will be given his father's land free of cost.[1] Paid in full
by the closest relative—the "redeemer."

For this is what redeemers do. They selflessly, sacrificially
give themselves for the well-being of their relatives. It's what God
requires family to do for family.

Will this be Ruth and Naomi's story? Will their closest relative
become their redeemer? If he says no, Boaz is next in line.

In the stillness of the night, Boaz told Ruth: "I will do for you all that you ask." Then his heart filled with praise for her. He knew she, too, was paying a high cost. She was sacrificing her own happiness. She could find a husband her own age and have a life of her own. But here she was, again, choosing to love God first— family first.

"Your kindness [chesedh] *tonight," Boaz said, "is greater than all you've done" (3:10, paraphrase).*

With that, he bestowed on her the greatest praise of all. In Hebrew the term is hayil. *It usually describes the most noble, wealthy, powerful people in Jewish society. It's reserved for war heroes and royalty, not for poor Moabite women. And yet, for Boaz, it perfectly described Ruth. She was a woman of nobility and excellence of character. He knew it. Everybody in town knew it.*

He said to her, "For all my people know that you are a 'hayil.'"[2]

Before morning's first light, Boaz filled her arms with as much food as she could carry. He would not let her go home to Naomi empty-handed. Then he assured her he would not let the sun set that day before her question to him was answered.

"If he will redeem you, good. But if he won't," Boaz promised, "I will."

And off she went, without anyone knowing she'd come to the threshing floor. In the same quiet way, Boaz made his way to the city gate where all legal transactions happened. He found the closest relative and, in front of the court, began to question him. Boaz was careful and shrewd. He presented his case like it was all about Naomi.

"Will you buy back her land?"

The man said yes, but nothing more.

Boaz pressed. He had to make sure this man was worthy of Ruth. Everybody knew about her. Did he? Did he know she was the best there was? That she had sacrificed everything for her family. Would he do that too? Would he pay the high cost of being her redeemer? Would he take her as his wife, raise up an heir, and do what God required family to do?

"I will not," the man said. "That would ruin me. You do it."

Boaz could have fought back and said, "Do your duty, man." But instead, he embraced the distinguished role of becoming her redeemer. And there, in the court of law, it all became official.

This great woman, this hayil, *would soon be his wife.*

"Really?" I said to Pastor Adams over the phone. "You'd let me come to a Wednesday night meeting of the Naomi Project?"

"If you behave," he teased, and at once I accepted.

I got there a few minutes early. The place was already packed. Louis and Charlotte had called and invited me to sit with them. "Third row, right side," he'd said, and that's exactly where I found them.

"You're gonna love tonight!" Louis beamed. And he was right. We spent a good deal of time in worship and Bible teaching. Pastor Adams spoke that night on 1 Timothy 3:5. I recorded the following words in my journal:

If you can't take care of your family—your spouse, your children, your elderly, your own—what makes you think God will let you care for His family? Or care for the people in our community?

Do it at home first. That's God's order in God's kingdom.

Give it out? First give it in. Don't give it in? You stay home!

It was a sobering message. "Faithful in first things," he kept thundering, as the people responded back, "Faithful in all things."

When he finished, Pastor Adams introduced a man nicknamed Hammer. Louis leaned over and said to me, "He's the best there is. He works with teenagers on the street—afternoons, weekends. He's rescued more kids for Christ than anyone I know."

"Hey, everybody," Hammer said in a deep, low voice. He looked to be in his midthirties. A bodybuilder with a shaved head and a large tattoo on the right side of his neck. "A week ago tonight," he started, "guess who shows up at my house? You want to see big, bad, and scary? That's what I saw!"

He waited for a second, let us think about it, and then pointed at Pastor Adams.

"I was gonna call the police," he said, as people laughed. "I invited him in but he just stood there on my front porch. He had that serious look on his face like I'd done something wrong. So, I asked him, 'What's going on?'

"He said, 'It's over, Hammer.'

"'What's over?' I asked him.

"'You know what I'm talking about.'

"'No, I don't,' I said. Next thing I know, my wife is standing next to me. She brings him inside, sits him down, and gets him something to drink. She's got that look in her eye like she knew he was coming—kids too. One minute, they're all over him, saying. 'Pastor has come to the house!' Next minute, they're gone. My wife is gone. It's just me and him, and he's staring at me.

"'Say what you gotta say,' I told him.

"'Already have,' he said.

"'All you've said is something's over. You're not talking about my work with the kids, are you?' Pastor nodded, and it felt like somebody whacked me across the face. He told me he knew my story, 'You work all day. Then you give everything you've got to the street kids. You give what's left over to your own kids, your wife, and others in your family. All that stops here, stops now.'

"Soon as I hear it, I go into bargaining mode. I told him, 'I'll do Tuesday, Friday, and Saturday. Smitty can have the rest. He's ready. But not this week, too much going on this week. As soon as I can, I will. You have my word on that.'

"Pastor shook his head and said, 'That's not what "it's over" means.'

"I told him he can't do this to me or to the kids on the street. But he said, 'Three months—then we'll talk.'

"I told him, 'These kids need me!'

"He said, 'If you mean your own kids, you got that right. Now spend time with them.' Then he stood up, went to the door to leave, and said, 'You know how it works, Hammer. Faithful in first things . . .' and then he turned and waited for me to say the rest. But I couldn't do it—not that night.

"So I stand here now," Hammer testified, "to tell you I'm stepping down from this ministry for a while. I need to confess my sin to you. I've not been faithful in first things. I've cared more for the street kids than my own kids. Some of you are going to need to take my place on the streets because I can't right now."

As he stepped away from the microphone, we all sat there in stunned silence. And then, one man stood, as if in standing he was honoring Hammer. And then another. Until everyone rose to their feet to honor the man who chose to honor God.

"That's Hammer!" Louis said, poking me in the side. "Didn't I tell you he's the best there is?"

QUESTIONS FOR REFLECTION

Here, at the end of Ruth, we see the cost of mercy. How do these words impact your life: *redeemer* and *hayil*?[3] How are you showing mercy to your family (see 1 Tim. 5:8)?

How are you being faithful in first things? Why did Hammer take his own family for granted? Do you? What needs to change in your life?

NOTES

1. The storyteller is combining the law (see Deut. 25:5–10) with the customs of the day (see Ruth 4:3–6). This same law came up in the New Testament when the Sadducees tested Jesus (see Matt. 22:23–33).

2. It is important to note we first see this word, *hayil*, describing Boaz in Ruth 2:1. It distinguishes him as a powerful, influential man in wealth and noble character. But for Ruth, a poor woman, *hayil* focuses on her character as a "woman of strength" and excellence (see Prov. 31:10). Robert L. Hubbard, *The Book of Ruth* (Grand Rapids, MI: Eerdmans, 1988), 133, 216.

3. In some Hebrew Bibles, the book of Ruth follows Proverbs. The "excellent wife" in Proverbs 31:10 (same Hebrew word, *hayil*) is then witnessed in the life of Ruth.

29

BORN TO SERVE

~~~

Reflections on Ruth 4:7–22

"A son has been born to Naomi!" So they named him Obed.
He is the father of Jesse, the father of David.

—RUTH 4:17

I try to picture the scene for myself. I imagine the baby snuggling soft against Naomi's neck and cooing. I see her gently rubbing his back, wondering if he'll fall asleep, but he doesn't. The little man is wide awake. She lifts him into the air, stares into his big bright eyes, and finds herself back in time. Back thirty years ago and more.

When she held her firstborn son.

Perhaps she and Elimelech were happy then. Can she still see him—like it was yesterday? Then, not long after, they welcomed a second son and, somehow, way too quickly, her little boys became handsome young men like their father, working the fields of Bethlehem, and finding favor with God.

Until the famine came.

She cradles the baby in her arm and smiles at him. He squeezes her finger and stretches his pudgy little legs. She holds him closer and, just as she starts to sing, I imagine her hearing the sound of people coming. Then a light tap sounds on the door.

"Naomi?" someone whispers, cracking the door slightly.

Naomi invites them in. These women are her friends, perhaps some since childhood. Perhaps the same who, on the day she returned from Moab dirty, poor, hungry, without husband, without sons, said in surprise, "Is this Naomi?" And all she could do was shake her head and say, "No, not anymore. Call me Bitter." For, back then, all she could feel deep in her soul was the Lord's anger against her (see Ruth 1:19–21).

Maybe one of the women sweeps the baby into her arms and gently bursts into joyful song. Soon enough, they all do, praising the Lord for Boaz, and for Ruth who loved Naomi more than seven sons, and then for the surprise blessing of this perfectly beautiful child.

"Blessed is the Lord," they sing, "who has not left you without a redeemer today, and may his name become famous in Israel."

And it was a surprise, wasn't it?

Ruth had been married to Mahlon for ten-plus years and had no children to show for it. In Israel, such a woman bears the reproach of barrenness. Now, in Bethlehem, how could it be expected that she would conceive a child?[1]

The storyteller tells us all we need to know: "And the LORD enabled her to conceive" (Ruth 4:13).

One of the women shouts, "A son has been born to Naomi." And she is right. Technically, Obed is both the surviving heir of her marriage with Elimelech and, at the same time, the heir of Mahlon and Ruth. It may sound awkward but Naomi is—according to Jewish Law—both mother and grandmother at the same time.

With that, the women spontaneously name the child Obed—a Hebrew word for "servant." Is it because they believed he'd come into the world to serve Naomi and heal her heart from all the grief she suffered? Perhaps.

But it's doubtful Naomi would have ever believed it. If anything, she'd be his nurse (4:16) and serve him because that's how *she lived life. It's what she did for her boys. It's what she did for Orpah and Ruth. And she'd do it again with Obed.*

She'd etch God's chesedh into his little heart. She'd teach him how to serve others more than himself. She's teach him the way of mercy and kindness. For this is her legacy. This is her family. It's Ruth. It's Boaz. And it still is her family to this day.

For from Obed came a king named David. And from David came the King of Kings whose name is also "Obed" or "Servant."[2] And from Him comes a new family down through all generations, all bearing the same family trait.

It's called mercy. It's called chesedh.

The church van arrived at my house a little before seven.

Every once in a while, Pastor Adams gets invited to share the story of the Naomi Project at church conferences. He never goes alone. This time, he asked if I'd like to go with him. "It's a Baptist church upstate," he told me.

The van was full. I got the last seat in the back.

I was surprised to sit next to Hammer. "Adams let you come?" I asked, telling him I'd been there the Wednesday night he spoke. He reminded me that four months had already passed. We talked together for the better part of an hour.

Then, all of a sudden we heard Pastor Adams shout, "We've got trouble!" Those in front of us gasped. There was a bad accident up ahead.

"Call 911," Adams ordered. "We've got no traffic, no emergency lights. This must've just happened. We're pulling over. Somebody start praying to Jesus."

"Pastor, if we stop, we'll be late," someone said, concerned.

"Not if we're on God's time," he said vehemently.

We came as close as we could to the accident and pulled to a stop. Adams turned to us and said, "You know what we do. We never pass by. We do what we can, where we can, when we can. This is our time. Go out there and let the Holy Spirit show you what to do." A second later, the van doors opened.

Immediately, I saw an SUV upside down with people trapped inside. There were two other cars—one back ended, the other badly damaged. We had with us an EMT and a nurse. They quickly took charge, assessing the scene. We discovered eight people in the accident. Three in the SUV were seriously injured, one critically. The other five had sustained either minor injuries or were just badly shaken up.

Each of us seemed to know what to do.

Some went to those with minor injuries. Some walked the perimeter of the accident praying. The rest of us attended the nurse and EMT at the SUV. Hammer and two other men pried open one of the car doors. The nurse started working on the most critically injured, while the EMT dealt with the other two.

"We've got a bleed. I need hands," the nurse called out.

I watched Pastor Adams get on his knees and crawl partway into the backseat. One hand on the bleed, the other holding the man's hand. The rest of us helped the EMT get the other passengers safely out of the SUV.

Within minutes, lights and sirens, medical teams, and police filled the space. With precision, the most critically injured were carefully extracted from the automobile. Then, in a well-orchestrated movement by trained professionals, the victims were rushed to the hospital by ambulance.

All within forty-five minutes of the accident.

After giving our statements to the police, we were back on the road. Pastor Adams had been scheduled to speak at 9:00. We didn't pull up to the conference until almost 11:00. By the time he actually got up to speak, it was 11:15.

"We're never late," he told the crowd, "when we're on God's time."

And with that, he began telling the story of Naomi and Ruth and Boaz and their beautiful son, Servant. "All these," he taught, "were in the line of the royal family that one day would birth the great King David, who would be the father of our Lord Jesus Christ, the Servant of all servants.

"Isn't that who we are supposed to be, too?" he challenged. As he described the Naomi Project, I sat back and marveled at the simplicity of it all. Is it possible that all the Lord requires of me is a willingness, an openness, to let Him, by His Holy Spirit, etch into my heart His heart—His *chesedh* heart?

And then, the rest will come. Easily, almost naturally. Just as Pastor Adams described so beautifully that day:

We have a saying at the Naomi Project: We never pass by. We do what we can, where we can, when we can.

Because Jesus didn't pass by.

So we walk the streets where God has placed us. To be merciful as He is merciful to us. For if He came to serve, then we come to serve.

Do you understand? This is our time, your time!
We never pass by.

QUESTIONS FOR REFLECTION

How do the words *servant* and *chesedh* shape the royal
family in Ruth? How does it shape your attitude, character,
and action as a Christian today?

Are you part of a Naomi Project in your church? Are
Christians being mobilized to take mercy into the local
community to do what we can, where we can, when we
can? If not, will you help start one?

NOTES

1. See Genesis 11:30; 16:1–3. Also, please note the insightful
work of Carolyn Custis James on the suffering of barrenness in Ruth,
in her book, *The Gospel of Ruth* (Grand Rapids, MI: Zondervan,
2008), 75–90.

2. The book of Ruth ends with a surprise: This is King
David's family! And, therefore, it is the gospel story of our Lord's
family. It should be noted that the beauty of the name Obed can
be seen in our Lord's character who came "not to be served, but
to serve, and to give His life a ransom for many" (Mark 10:45).

PART 5

THE BRILLIANT LAWYER

30

HE KNOWS EVERYTHING!

Reflections on Luke 10:21–28

And a lawyer stood up and put Him to the test, saying,
"Teacher, what shall I do to inherit eternal life?" And He said to
him, "What is written in the Law? How does it read to you?"

—LUKE 10:25–26

The lawyer sat there waiting. Perhaps irritated.

And why not? For the last while, Jesus had been meeting with His disciples. He'd sent them out. Now they were back—all ecstatic and happy—saying they had performed miracles. He thought he heard Jesus say, "I saw Satan fall from heaven!"

What kind of person says something like that?

Then he heard Jesus pray, "Thank You, Father. You hide these things from the wise and reveal them to little children!" What did He mean by that? Was he talking about him in particular? This had to stop.

"Teacher!" he said, standing up.

One word and he had Jesus' attention, just like he'd hoped. As Jesus moved toward him, the lawyer said, "Answer me this: What must I do to inherit eternal life?"

It was the perfect question. How would Jesus answer him? Would He point to God? Would He point to the law of Moses and say publicly that life after death is granted only to those who keep the commandments of God? Or would He point to himself? That was the gossip on the street, that he said what no one should ever say: "You must follow [not the law! Not the teaching of the elders!]—Me!"

The lawyer had to hear it for himself.

But Jesus was shrewd. He came closer. He volleyed questions back. "What does the law say?" And then, more pointedly, "How do you read it?" Which was exactly how the lawyer's colleagues would have responded. They'd spar and debate, formulating their arguments—especially against the Sadducees.[1] But how does he respond now to Jesus? Is He expecting the wisdom of "little children"? Well, if He wants a child's answer, He'll get a child's answer.

"To love the Lord your God," he recited. "With all your heart, soul, strength, and mind. To love your neighbor as yourself."

"You've got it!" Jesus exclaimed. "Perfect answer!" No doubt trying to make the lawyer feel like he knew everything there was to know.

But the lawyer is clearly agitated. He decides to put more pressure on Jesus. This was not over.

But before he could speak, Jesus commanded the moment. He said what nobody had ever said before—ever. Not the priests. Not the prophets. Not the rabbis of ages past. Not the scholars of his own day. This was not a child's response. It was more complicated than that. It was confusing to the lawyer. It was beyond him—way beyond him. "Do this!" Jesus urged. "And that life— that eternal life—is yours right now!"[2]

I sat outside the bishop's office waiting for him.

It was the fall of 1985. I was in my second year of seminary. I'd been born into and raised in the Episcopal Church.

My uncle had been a priest, then bishop, and I'm sure that influenced my desire as a child to become a pastor too.

But evidently, I had "trouble" written all over me.

I belonged (as we said in those days) to a very "evangelical" Episcopal church. The Bible was preached as the Word of God. People were coming to saving faith in Jesus. In fact, so many were coming, the church had to rent out the local high school to fit everybody. I simply loved it. I always had the sense the Lord was there—presiding in His church and wanting us to receive the fullness of His Spirit to worship Him. To serve Him. And to tell others about Him.

It made me want to be a pastor all the more.

And so, with the church's blessing, I met with the bishop for the first time in the summer of 1984. I quickly learned he didn't like our church much—not exactly. He told me if I was to be ordained to the pastorate, I'd have to attend a seminary of his choosing. Because, he said, I needed to be broadened.

Apparently I was too narrow as an "evangelical," too rigid, in how I perceived the world.

Not knowing how to take this, my wife and I went to our pastor for counsel. "Do what the bishop says," he advised. "Go to seminary, learn it all—just be careful not to believe it all. Trust the Lord will help you."

So off I went—nervous, if I were to be candid.

After my first year of seminary, I spent the summer of 1985 in a hospital chaplaincy program. This was required for all pastors in training.

And I had done well. Really well.

So, that fall, when the bishop called me to come to his office to meet with him, I was, perhaps, overconfident. If anything, I was annoyed. It had taken almost two hours to get to his office due to horrible rains and a huge backup on the highway because of an accident. Thankfully, I'd left in plenty of time. I got to the bishop's office without a minute to spare.

And then sat there—for over an hour.

This was not going well. When he finally opened the door and called me, I did my best to compose myself and be gracious. He led the way into his office, stepped behind his desk, and sat down. I found a chair in front.

"No need to sit," he barked.

"Bishop?"

For a few minutes he did his best with small talk. He asked about my family. He wanted to know what classes I was taking. His manner was abrupt and businesslike, and I kept my answers to a minimum. Finally, he put his reading glasses down, leaned forward in his chair, and looked right at me.

"I didn't want to say this over the phone. I know you did your hospital chaplaincy this past summer. You're going to do it again. Next summer."

He paused, waiting for my reaction.

"Why? I thought I did well."

He didn't respond. He just kept staring at me.

When I nodded and told him I'd do it, the meeting ended. He told me to apply to the state mental hospital chaplaincy program and keep him informed. He then put on his glasses and resumed working at his desk.

He was done with me.

Actually, I was done with him too. I didn't say it out loud, but I was angry. Nobody in my seminary class had to repeat summer chaplaincy. Why me? It felt like the bishop was punishing me for being part of a church he didn't like. It was totally unfair. And, clearly, I had no option but to do what he said.

So I applied to the program.

In early spring, they accepted me, and I began working at the state mental hospital in mid-June 1986. There were six of us in the program. During the days of orientation, I met privately with the supervisor.

"Do you know why I'm here?" I asked him.

Leslie was a tall, thin man in his early sixties with a kind, gentle manner. He'd been a pastor for years and, midcareer, made the change to chaplaincy. I could tell it suited him well. He had a kind of presence that engendered trust. He looked at me, surprised. "Yes, I do. You mean you don't?"

I shook my head.

"Well, why you do think?"

"Not sure the bishop likes me all that much."

"No," he said, definitively. "That's not the impression I got."

I gazed out his office window at the deep blue summer sky. I wanted to be anywhere but here. Most of my colleagues were doing summer internships at churches. Others had jobs to bring in some needed cash for their families during these lean school years. Me—well, I simply felt sorry for myself.

Leslie looked down at his notes. "He's concerned about you. He wants you to experience those difficult places in life where we don't have all the answers, where we can't quote a Bible verse and make all our problems go away. He wants you to know more about the suffering in this world."

"What?" I said, indignant.

"Yeah," he said, looking at me like he understood what the bishop meant. And then he said words that stole the breath from my body: "The bishop thinks you might know everything there is to know. He'd like to change that."

QUESTIONS FOR REFLECTION

If "eternal life" comes by saving grace, why does Jesus command us to "do" the love commands? In what way does eternal life start now?

How does arrogance come into our souls? Is it possible we think we know everything there is to know? What needs to change inside us?

NOTES

1. The lawyer believed eternal life is real and inheritable through the things we do. The Sadducees, in contrast, did not believe in the resurrection to come or life after death. See Luke 20:27.

2. Our Lord put the conversation of eternal life into a whole new framework. He announced that it's more than what happens after death. It begins, for those who believe in Him and live the love commands, here and now.

31

CLUELESS

~~~

Reflections on Luke 10:29

*But wishing to justify himself, he said to Jesus,
"And who is my neighbor?"*

—LUKE 10:29

*If this was a formal debate, the lawyer lost the opening round.
He knew that. He had set a trap for Jesus, and it didn't work.
Instead, Jesus pushed back. Hard. Strong. With words the lawyer
didn't understand. So what does he do next?*

*Should he ask Him, "What do You mean eternal life begins
now?"*

*No, if he did that, Jesus would have the advantage. He could
make a fool out of him in front of everybody and say something
like, "How is it you're a teacher in Israel and don't understand
these things?" (see John 3:10).*

Maybe he should just sit down.

*Or maybe not. Debate was the lawyer's expertise. It was his
gift from God. If Jesus was, as many of his colleagues suspected,
a false prophet, then He would never withstand the force, the
power, of his logic. The lawyer, after all, had Scripture. He had
wisdom from God. He had years of experience in the courtroom.
He had what he needed most—confidence.*

He chose to attack again.

But on what grounds? He decided not to reengage the question of eternal life. It was best to attack from a position of strength and certainty. A debate he'd win. And better still—one that would strike at the heart of where Jesus had gone wrong. And He had gone wrong, completely wrong, on this question of "neighbor."

Jesus willfully violated the teaching of the elders. The lawyer knew—everybody knew—God defined "neighbor" as the Jewish people. Not those outside Israel. And even then it must be Jews who were real Jews walking in obedience to God and His law. This was the accepted teaching.

But not to Jesus.

From the streets to the synagogues, He was known as a glutton. A drunkard. A friend of sinners (see Luke 7:34). And it was obviously true. No doubt the crowd around him that day was full of prostitutes, Jewish tax collectors, and the dregs of society—all followers of Jesus. Who here even qualified as "neighbor" in God's eyes? This, the lawyer decided, was where he would take his stand.

If Jesus even tried to defend himself, saying He agreed with the elders' teaching, He'd lose at once. He'd have to explain this crowd around Him and He couldn't. No, He was trapped here. The fact was, He was a false prophet, living in rebellion to the proper interpretation of Scripture. He was misleading the people.

It was time to expose Him.

The lawyer made his move. He may have lost the first round, but he would win this one. He would justify himself in front of everybody. There would be vindication. All he had to do was speak the words out loud. The crowd might not get it. But Jesus would. He would feel the justice of God hemming Him in from every side. There would be no escape.

"Poor Jesus," the lawyer must have thought, "so powerful yet so clueless."

The crowd was quiet. The words came easily, smoothly, with more confidence than he expected: "Who is my neighbor?" (Luke 10:29).

My first week as chaplain at the state mental hospital flew by.

The bishop had asked Leslie, my supervisor, to assign me to a ward with lower-functioning patients. I spent a good chunk of the day with them, and the rest with Leslie and my classmates as we processed our various experiences.

My attitude was not good.

I was still angry at the bishop. I felt judged by him. He'd put me in this little tiny box and stamped a label on me: "narrow" or "evangelical." And why? Was it because he was offended by what was happening in our church? Was he really opposed to our pastors calling people to saving faith in Christ? But why didn't he like it? It made no sense to me. And why was he taking it out on me, consigning me to an entire summer at this wretched hospital? Really?

I tried to hide my anger. But during the second week of the program, it popped out unexpectedly. One of my classmates was leading a Bible study. He asked us to join in and talk about it together. As we did, I heard something I didn't like. I felt he wrongly understood a particular Bible verse.

So I broke in and corrected him.

He looked at me puzzled. They all did.

"You're wrong about this," he chided. He gave his explanation, others chimed in, and I soon realized—they were right. I'd misunderstood.

I apologized.

Somehow my anger, my bad attitude, had left me cold and uncaring to my fellow classmates. One of them spontaneously belted out, "I can't believe how arrogant you are." Again, I apologized—as sincerely as I could. I looked over at Leslie, hoping to gain his support. But his head was down. He was writing notes on his legal pad. My heart instantly sank.

This would get back to my bishop.

Once again, I'd be branded with words like *arrogant* and *self-righteous*.

I resolved to do better. It was still early in the summer. I had time on my side. I'd stumbled, yes. But hopefully, not for long. I'd do my best with the patients. I'd work hard to gain my classmates' respect. I'd promise Leslie I'd never let this happen again.

I'd make sure of it.

A few days later, I had my weekly meeting with Leslie. I was nervous about it. I was convinced—first words out of his mouth—he'd bring up the incident at the Bible study. I was afraid he too had labeled me. And more afraid he and the bishop had already talked. That thought had kept me awake for a few nights.

But instead, as always, Leslie surprised me. He instantly put me at ease. "Tell me how it's going for you so far," he said, concerned.

"Not great," I replied bluntly.

"That's what I thought."

"I have to do well this summer, and I feel like I'm already failing miserably."

"In what way?"

"I need the bishop's approval—which means I have to do more than simply pass this program. I did that last summer. I have to somehow meet his expectations, and I don't know what they are or how to do it."

"So that's your focus, is it?" Leslie asked. "You have to make sure the bishop's happy with you?"

"If I don't he won't ordain me."

"Seems odd to me," Leslie reflected, writing something on his pad.

"What's that?"

"Well, you're obviously angry with him. He's forcing you to be here and you, clearly, don't want to be. If I were you, I'd want to defend myself. Make an appointment, go see him, and prove him wrong. But you can't. You need his approval too badly. So you're stuck here—with me!"

And then he smiled, comfortably.

"That's about it!" I volleyed back, trying to be cheerful.

"And what would you tell him if you could?"

"That he's judged me wrongly, without even knowing me. He's done the same with our church. I feel like he marginalizes those who openly talk about Jesus Christ and what He's done for us. We get pigeonholed, and I don't understand it. Is he as clueless about the Christian faith as he is about me?"

Leslie let my words hang in the air for a minute.

"So what are you going to do about it?"

"I don't know. Maybe you could help?"

"How?"

"Maybe you could call him? Ask him what he wants from me?"

Leslie shook his head. "That's not my job." And then he looked at me with sadness in his eyes. As if I'd hurt him somehow. As if it was me, not the bishop, who was the most clueless.

"Do you know why I'm here?" he asked. "God gave me a heart for the people who live day in and day out at this hospital. And I help train chaplains who have the same heart. That's my job. And right now, I think it's pretty clear, that's not you. Your heart is somewhere else and, to be honest, that's not acceptable. You being here, with that attitude, isn't working for me."

QUESTIONS FOR REFLECTION

How do you define *neighbor*? Have you ever tried to justify yourself for not loving people that you're certain God doesn't love either?

In this story, I am blinded by anger and unable to see the people on the ward. When have you been clueless to the people God, in His mercy, has given you to love?

32

PASSING BY

Reflections on Luke 10:30–32

*And by chance a priest was going down
on that road, and when he saw him, he passed
by on the other side. Likewise a Levite also.*

—LUKE 10:31–32

The mood has shifted. One minute Jesus was rejoicing "greatly in the Holy Spirit" (Luke 10:21). The next the lawyer's on the attack. He demanded answers. He was convinced Jesus' definition of "neighbor" put Jesus in direct opposition to God's Word.

Why did Jesus even respond to him? Why didn't He simply dismiss him by saying what He'd said before, "Love your enemies, do good to those who hate you" (Luke 6:27)?

Instead, He has compassion on the lawyer. He decides to tell him a story that could possibly heal his dark, twisted soul.

"A man . . ." He began, loud enough for the crowd to hear.

He didn't give the man a name. No country of origin. Was he Roman? Was he Jewish? Was he educated? Wealthy or poor? Young or old? Was he living a moral life—blameless before God and the elders of His people? Jesus didn't say. He gave no facts—making it impossible for His hearers to assess whether this man was worthy of being called "neighbor."

He told only this: The man was traveling the road from Jerusalem to Jericho and "fell among robbers, and they stripped him and beat him, and went away leaving him half dead" (Luke 10:30). This was common, everyday news. It happened all the time. Of all roads, this one was among the most dangerous. Thieves, bandits, men of evil would lurk in shadows, attack at random, and beat their victims senseless.[1]

And there he was—bloodied, naked, beyond recognition.

Why not end the story here? All Jesus needed to do was ask the lawyer, "How about this man? Will you love him as your neighbor?"

But no, He kept going. He decided to press and press hard. In a stunning move—bold, confrontational, and intensely personal—a priest appeared in the story. He was walking the same road. Breathing the same air. And finding himself only a few feet away from the beaten man, who lay there barely alive. He saw him with his own eyes.

Of all people—a priest. A man of equal standing with the lawyer.[2]

And what did the priest do? Did he love this man as his neighbor? No, he did not.

To make matters worse, another man passed by. This time, a Levite. All of them—priest, Levite, lawyer—they were all colleagues and peers. They were men of highest reputation in Jewish society. They were educated by the greatest scholars of their time. They were responsible before God to know His law and teach it to the people of Israel. So how did these great men handle the question, "Who is my neighbor?" in real life, real time, when he was lying in front of them bloodied and half dead?

They did nothing. They passed him by.

If only Jesus had stopped the story right there, got into the lawyer's face, and asked in disgust, "Who does this? What kind of person leaves him there to die?" The obvious answer is this: No one does. No one passes by.

And how much worse if it's a priest, a Levite, or a lawyer? Jesus' message is clear: "You people know the right answer, but you have no idea what it means."

"I'll do better," I immediately promised Leslie.

He looked out his office window and thought for a moment. I watched as he slowly shook his head, looked back at me, and said, "I don't think so. You're too driven by performance, and I'm not interested. I think we're done here."

"Excuse me?"

"I don't want you in the program."

I sat there in silence like he'd smacked me across the face and hit me so hard I couldn't even feel it yet. My first thought—he didn't mean it. Maybe he was testing me. But the pain started, a hot searing pain in my heart, as tears flooded my eyes. Everything I'd worked for these past few years suddenly felt like it was crashing down on top of me.

"But I have to stay," I whispered, afraid my voice wasn't stable.

Leslie never took his eyes off mine. His face kind and compassionate. His eyes soft and understanding. He made no effort to speak—not at first.

"OK, I'll tell you what," he finally said, almost whispering back. "Tomorrow is Friday. Take the day off. Go home, talk with your wife, and say your prayers. If you're back here on Monday, I'll know it's because you want God's heart for the people here—to love them more than you love yourself. Is that a deal?"

I nodded and thanked him. But what he said stung.

"He's right," I told Erilynne when I got home that night. "I don't want to be there. When I'm on the floor with the patients, I'm just doing my job, watching the clock, and wishing I was somewhere else—anywhere else. I treat the patients like they're patients, not people. I don't love them, not like I should."

The more we talked, the more I realized how cold my heart had become.

Later that night, as we prayed together, Erilynne felt like we should go back to our pastor and talk to him. So we went to him after church that Sunday.

His reaction surprised us. "Well, as hard as this is to hear," he said with a smile, "I think it's good news. It sounds to me like you're at this hospital by divine appointment. The Lord has clearly set apart this place, this time, and these people to do a work in your heart. So here's my question: Are you willing and ready?"

"I hadn't thought about it like that," I confessed.

"I didn't think so. And that may be part of the problem."

We both looked at him, confused.

"If being at this hospital is, in fact, God's plan for your life, then you need to understand something: The bishop was right about you. He prayed, heard from God, and followed His lead. He is for you, not against you. Once you accept this, you'll find a new freedom to embrace this summer in ways you've never dreamed. The Lord has something in mind here. If I were you, I'd find out what it is."

No! I wanted to protest, not wanting to let go of my anger against the bishop. Are you kidding? This summer is God's plan for my life? But somehow I knew he was right.

"I think I agree," Erilynne said, looking straight at me.

"I guess I do too," I said, nodding. Then our pastor put his arms around us and prayed my heart would change toward the bishop, the summer program, and each person on my hospital ward.

It was exactly what I needed. On Monday morning, before I left for the hospital, Erilynne and I prayed it again. We asked the Lord to give me His love for Leslie, my classmates, and the people on my floor.

"I'm glad you're back," Leslie said when I got there. He kindly reached out his hand to welcome me. "How was the weekend?"

"Hard," I said, honestly. "But good."

"Are you ready to talk about it with the class?"

"Not really, but yes, I will."

He smiled and said, "I was hoping you'd say that."

And I did. A little later that morning, when we were all together, I told them everything—including my last conversation with Leslie. "He asked me not to come back, and he was right to say it. I came here with the wrong attitude. My heart, my focus, hasn't been here with you or Leslie or the people in this hospital. I need to say to each of you I am sorry and ask your forgiveness."

"So what changed?" Leslie prompted.

"My wife and I met with our pastor after church yesterday. He helped us see that it's God's will for me to be here.

If that's true, then I have a lot to learn—from my bishop, from you all, and from the people on my floor."

Leslie looked at my classmates and asked them to respond. Thankfully, they were more than gracious. They thanked me for my honesty and offered their help. It couldn't have gone better.

"What about you?" one of my classmates asked Leslie, almost as a tease. "Are you going to let him stay?"

"I think so," Leslie replied with a more serious tone than I expected. "For now, he has the right answer. But only time will tell if he has the right heart."

QUESTIONS FOR REFLECTION

Discuss Jesus' compassion and mercy for this lawyer? Why make him see his colleagues pass by the beaten man? How does this speak to you?

I needed both a change of mind and a change of heart. Why is it so hard for us to change? When has the Lord worked these kinds of changes in you?

NOTES

1. Joel B. Green wrote in his commentary on Luke, "Realistic, too, is the picture of violence on the road, since travel in general—and especially travel on this particular road—was replete with danger" (*The Gospel of Luke* [Grand Rapids, MI: Eerdmans, 1997], 430).

2. The lawyer in this story could well have been a priest, since "priests functioned as experts on the law, when not performing their priestly duties at the temple" (Ibid., 427). The two men are almost indistinguishable.

33

SAM

Reflections on Luke 10:33

*But a Samaritan, who was on a journey, came upon him;
and when he saw him, he felt compassion.*

—LUKE 10:33

Why didn't Jesus end the story?

He answered the lawyer's question. He said in effect, "That man on the side of the road, beaten senseless, is your neighbor. It doesn't matter who people are or what they've done. Go love them!"

Next, He accused him. The picture of the priest and Levite passing by the body with no mercy accomplished that. It's why He said countless times before to people just like the lawyer, "You preach but you do not practice" (see Matt. 23:2–3). Right doctrine means nothing when you do nothing.

Why wasn't that enough?

But it wasn't. Jesus had more work to do in caring for this lawyer's soul. He decided to press harder this time. He had to confront the prejudice in the man's heart.

Another character entered the story.

Down the same road. Breathing the same air. Seeing the same half-dead body. But this man was different. This man had compassion. He was unable to leave the beaten man there in his suffering. He had to do something about it. He had to, for the greatness and power of the second commandment was alive in him.

And that was the point of Jesus' teaching on the two Great Commandments (10:27).

He wasn't talking about philanthropists who care for the less fortunate.[1] He was talking about those who embrace the first commandment to the fullest. For it's only when we love God with everything we are that He fills our hearts with love for others and for ourselves. Experience the first, and the second comes to life!

So here he stands. And he wasn't just any man without description. He was a Samaritan.

For the lawyer, what could be worse? Samaritans were outcasts, rejected by God. This was the teaching of the lawyers, priests, and Levites. They believed Samaritans were wrong about God. Wrong in their view of Scripture. Wrong in how they worshiped. Wrong in every way about everything. They did not qualify as neighbors (John 4:9).

And that, for Jesus, was unacceptable.

For this reason, He forced the lawyer to stare into the Samaritan's face. If he wanted to hate him—fine! But for now, he would have to watch him. Watch him as he took notice of the man on the side of the road. Watch him as compassion filled his heart. Watch him go and do what the priest and Levite refused to go and do.

The Samaritan loved as a neighbor is supposed to love his neighbor.

Poor Mr. Right had to watch Mr. Wrong do what was right.

And here, if we could freeze the frame, we might ask at this point, did the lawyer understand what was happening here? Did he have any idea that just as the Samaritan was caring for this man's broken body so our Lord was caring for him and his broken soul?

These stories are one and the same. Same mercy. Same compassion. Two men needing the same rescue.

That week, I focused on the patients.

Or rather, *people*.

You see, that was my problem. Every time I entered the ward, I felt a rush of anxiety. I knew nothing about mental illness. It was easier for me to shadow the doctors, nurses, and aides. I'd ask all kinds of questions, take copious notes, and, occasionally, read medical charts (when they'd let me). Then, after they left, I'd sit with the patients and observe them through the lens of their illness.

I hate admitting it, but it was safer that way.

That week, I resolved to change all that. I made three calculated decisions. I stopped hiding behind the staff. I stopped thinking of the people as "patients." And I started honoring each person with the love and dignity they deserved.

Great plan—it just didn't work very well.

Being on my own was hard. I found some people wanted nothing to do with me and told me so. Some simply walked away the moment I approached. Others let me sit with them but ignored me. And while others latched on, talked a mile a minute as if we were best friends and then, later in the day, turned on me for no apparent reason. My brilliant new strategy was an utter disaster.

I needed to find people who wanted me in their space.

People I could impact for the better.

Of the thirty people on the ward, I soon identified eight as being the most accessible. They didn't mind having me around. A few seemed to enjoy it. So, I decided I'd spend the rest of the summer—the remaining two and a half months—caring for them. I'd see them as my summer family.

Not that I wouldn't pray for the rest—or visit the rest (as they'd let me). But I'd invest myself—my time, my gifts, my heart—into these eight people.

"How's it going for you?" Leslie asked at our weekly meeting.

"Pretty well," I responded cheerfully. I told him about the changes I'd made. When I mentioned the eight people in particular, he registered surprise.

I stopped and asked, "Is something wrong?"

"Why these eight? Why not the others?" he inquired.

"They respond to me. I think I can make a difference in their lives."

"Is that why you're here?"

"I'd like to think so."

Leslie shook his head but stayed quiet. I knew I'd upset him.

"If I can win their trust—day after day, week after week," I stated, "I can do something for them. I can bring help in their lives. Even hope. Maybe pray with them. Maybe the Lord would use me this summer to make their lives better."

"What if it doesn't work?" he asked curtly.

"I'm hoping it will."

"What if you make no difference at all? What if, on the day after you leave, no one on that ward even knows you're gone? No one misses you? No one even remembers your name? And what if they're exactly the same—no change from when you first met them at the beginning of summer. How will you feel then?"

I couldn't answer him.

"It's hard for you, isn't it?" Leslie observed, leaning toward me. "You have to make a difference in people's lives. For them—yes. But—for yourself. It makes you feel better about you if you make people feel better about them. Isn't that right? And sometimes in life, that's not how it works."

"But I'd like it to work," I said slowly, trying to respond. "I can't imagine being in a world where I make no impact at all—on anybody."

Leslie nodded and said, "I believe that's why you're here."

"What?" I reacted, and then I remembered. At our first meeting, Leslie told me the bishop wanted me to experience people in suffering—real suffering—where I could do nothing about it. I couldn't fix them. I couldn't quote a Bible verse or give godly counsel that would rescue their situation or ease their pain. I'd have to learn to stay there with them. Powerless and compassionate.

I nodded and simply said, "OK."

"Then change your strategy," Leslie directed. "Love the thirty equally. Not just the eight. Is that clear?"

"Yes, sir, it is."

"And if you don't know how to do that, ask the Lord to help you."

I thanked him and, before heading home for the weekend, made my way back to the ward. I wanted to go to the game room and just sit for a while. Most of the thirty people were there—just hanging out, watching TV, doing what they did every afternoon before their 5:00 dinner. And, as usual, no one seemed to notice me. I'd become, as I now understood, invisible and insignificant. And I felt it.

"Hey, there," a man said as he sat down next to me. He was dressed casually—like everybody on the ward. Not recognizing him, I assumed he was a new aide.

"You're going to be all right," he assured me. "I'll see to it."

"Excuse me?"

"Call me Sam," he answered. "And don't worry about anything. I know what's going on here, and I'll make sure things go better for you. I promise you that."

He shook my hand, and somehow I believed him.

QUESTIONS FOR REFLECTION

In what ways are the lawyer and the half-dead man similar? And what about Jesus and the Samaritan? Where are you in this story?

Like the lawyer, I had no idea I was in need of rescue. How do we love as Jesus calls us to love? How do we bring dignity and honor to each person?

NOTE

1. The secular world defines good Samaritans as people who help those in need without making any reference to God. And yet, the actual story of the Samaritan is impossible to understand without God at the center, without Him as the source of real love and real mercy. Our Lord makes the two commands inseparable, the second ever dependent on the first.

34
METICULOUS MERCY

Reflections on Luke 10:34–35

*[A Samaritan] came to him and bandaged up his wounds, pouring oil
and wine on them; and he put him on his own beast, and brought
him to an inn and took care of him. On the next day he took out two
denarii and gave them to the innkeeper and said, "Take care of
him; and whatever more you spend, when I return I will repay you."*

—LUKE 10:34–35

*Here it is—mercy! Mercy in its splendor and glory. Mercy in
meticulous detail. Mercy for the lawyer to see—for us all to see.*

*Just watch the Samaritan. He stopped his travels. He saw the
man, felt compassion course through his veins, and did what
mercy always does. He acted. He left his donkey, went to the man,
assessed his condition, and began the work. He had everything
he needed to treat him: oil and wine.*

*It was the only medicine he had. Freely he poured—washing,
cleansing, anointing—gently tending each wound and then
wrapping it carefully in clean cloth before going to the next. One
at a time. It took time. Mercy always takes time.*

There were no words between them.

*The man was still, no doubt unconscious. The Samaritan
knew he couldn't leave him there. He needed a plan. He had to
take him somewhere. But how could he do it? How could he get
the beaten man—this dead weight—up off the ground and onto
his donkey with as little trauma as possible? Nobody else seemed
to be around to help.*

He figured out a way—compassion and mercy are surprising that way.

He secured the man safely on his donkey and began the journey. Slowly—step by step. He knew an inn. He knew the innkeeper. With each step, he reordered his life. The plans he had, the places he needed to be, the people he needed to meet, the well-being of his business and family—all put on hold.

He got to the inn and booked a room. He decided to spend the night.

He couldn't leave him—not then. The man needed care.

In the morning, he met with the innkeeper. He booked the room again, and again, for as long as it took. He had no interest in asking the innkeeper to share the expense for the care of this stranger. He wanted to pay for it, all of it. Mercy—real mercy— always costs. Always gives. Always sacrifices.

There was trust between him and the innkeeper. There had to be.

Like old friends, they easily entered a business deal where money was exchanged. The Samaritan advanced him two days' wages and said in effect, "Care for him! Spend what you will, put it on my tab, and when I come back, I will pay it in full!" The innkeeper took the money, assuring his promise to care for the man.

And as he did, our Lord ended the story.

A good story. The man lived! Mercy came. Mercy broke through the powers of evil that assaulted him and breathed life into his nearly dead body. Mercy, in meticulous detail, through this man from Samaria who gave his all—his time, his money, his heart—to love this stranger as his neighbor.

The poor, tormented lawyer. How would he react to Jesus? Would his heart harden, hating any story where a Samaritan is a hero? Or would it soften?

This was his moment. Mercy was standing right in front of him, loving him as a neighbor is meant to be loved.

The next few weeks, I did exactly what Leslie said: "Love the thirty equally."

The only way to do this with integrity, I decided, was to leave my "tool belt" home. I wasn't there to fix anybody's problems. Not anymore. I made sure, in the course of a week, I spent time with each person. If they didn't want me around, I stayed at a distance. I had no agenda but to simply be with them.

I must say, I missed my tool belt.

There was suffering on this ward. Every day—unchanging. With tools, I could focus on solutions. Without them, all that was left was to be with these people in their suffering today. And again, tomorrow. With no hope they'd be better. No chance we could set goals, see improvement, and take steps forward.

Not here. Halfway through the summer, I wrote this in my journal:

Each day, despair grows deeper. I don't know how to love when I can't help. Is that wrong? All my life I've lived in a world where love and hope are inseparably bound. Who cares if something's broken? We fix it. We change the story. We believe that with God, all things are possible.

But here it's different.

The longer I stay, the more afraid I get. This could be me. I could be suffering like any person here. This ward could be my home for the rest of my life. I try not to think about it. But when I do, it makes me want to run.

Instead, I force myself to stay. I ask what I have to ask—if I were any one of these people today, how would I want to be treated? Honored? Loved?

Lord Jesus Christ, show me how to love each person equally.

That simple prayer was answered quickly.

Sam.

He was not an aide. He'd been living at the hospital for seventeen years. With his condition worsening, a doctor decided to transfer him to our ward.

And he was extraordinary. He knew exactly how to love everybody on the floor—fully. Whether he was loved back or not, he didn't seem to care. There was no question he favored the underdog. The moment somebody got hurt or cried or lost their temper, he ran to help them. But he cared for the bully as much as for those being bullied. And rarely did I see anyone care for him in return.

One day, I wrote about him in my journal:

He's the tissue guy—two criers this morning. He got there first.

Watched a young man throw his juice cup against the wall. Sam cleaned it up and got him more juice.

When I got in this morning, he was making beds with the aides.

*I love watching him care for the "loners"—he knows
exactly what to do.*

*Nurse slammed down the phone in anger. Sam saw
it and went to her. He grabbed her hand and told her
she looked pretty today.*

*Guy shoved him hard. Sam didn't shove back—
instead, he apologized.*

*At the cafeteria. he bussed everybody's dishes—with
no thanks.*

And every day, sometimes twice a day, he'd check up on
me. "You're better now, aren't you? I can tell, you know!"
he'd say. Or, "You're right where you're supposed to be. Don't
forget that. It's all part of the plan!" Or maybe he'd just buzz
by, pat my shoulder, smile, and give me a thumbs-up sign.

"Sam, you're the best!" I'd call out.

He'd shake his head and reply, "No, I'm not."

The sad part about Sam was his cough. It was loud and
guttural. Often it came in spasms, and when it started, he
couldn't stop it. Those around him, of course, reacted.
They'd yell at him. Force him to leave the room. Call him
names. I know it hurt him. But I also could tell the coughing
scared him.

I went to his doctor and asked her about it. She
explained it was a side effect of long-term use of his med-
ication. She added there was no treatment for it. "He'll
most likely die from this," she said. "It will continue to get
worse, and his heart can only take so much."

"You mean there's nothing you can do?"

She shook her head.

And that, for me, broke my heart. Of all the people I've met through all my years, I've rarely seen someone like Sam. He knows how to love without being loved back. He has no need for a tool belt. He's not out to fix anybody. He simply allows the kingdom of God to burst onto the floor in acts of mercy, kindness, and love. And I, for the summer, got to be his student.

"Guess who I love?" he asked me one late afternoon.

"I think you love just about everybody," I remarked.

"Guess again," he pressed.

"Who?"

"Jesus!" he exclaimed, with a smile big and bright. "And guess what?" he persisted.

"What?" I said, pretending like he was bothering me. And with that, he put his arm around my shoulder and gave me a gentle hug. In almost a whisper, he told me everything I needed to know about him.

"He loves me back!"

QUESTIONS FOR REFLECTION

How did the Lord Jesus rescue you? How does He still rescue you? How do you describe His mercy to you in the same kind of meticulous detail that the Samaritan showed to the wounded man?

What prevents us from showing mercy and love unconditionally to everyone around us? Why can't we do for others what Jesus has done for us?

35

THY KINGDOM COME

Reflections on Luke 10:36–37

*"Which of these three do you think proved to be a
neighbor to the man who fell into the robbers' hands?"
And he said, "The one who showed mercy toward him."
Then Jesus said to him, "Go and do the same."*

—LUKE 10:36–37

*Of all the preachers who've ever lived, of all the sermons ever
preached, no one had ever explained the two Great Commandments
like this.*

And Jesus did it here, with him—a gift to the brilliant lawyer.

*With it came a simple question. It wasn't designed to trick
him or embarrass him or give even the slightest possible chance
he might get it wrong. He wouldn't get it wrong. A child could
answer it.*

*But it's the most important question of all. It's not, "Do you
believe in God's mercy?" But rather, "Who in this story lived God's
mercy?"*

*Why this question? The beaten man needed more than
someone who believed the command to "love your neighbor."
He needed someone who lived it. Otherwise, he would die. So
who did? Who let God's love explode through him? Who let
mercy triumph over evil? Who rescued this man who fell prey to
robbers and, by so doing, proved himself to be a neighbor by
loving his neighbor?*

Was it the priest—did he do it?

How about the Levite—was it him?

Or, maybe the Samaritan?

One of these three men was so filled with the first commandment that, as soon as he saw the man's beaten body, he let the second commandment pour through him with all his heart, soul, strength, and mind.

"Tell me, which one was it?" Jesus asked him.

The lawyer had options. He didn't have to answer. He could have stayed quiet. Or he could have picked up his stuff and left. Or he could have answered by not answering, by changing the subject, by arguing and debating in defense of the priest and Levite. He did none of these things. Instead, he gave the answer: "Of the three, it's the one who showed mercy."

Even then, he couldn't say the word *Samaritan*. Even after hearing the story of the Samaritan, he wouldn't let the word pass by his lips. For though the Samaritan may have been the real neighbor, the real hero, in the story, there was a prejudice inside the lawyer. Samaritans were not "neighbors." Never had been. Never would be.

Jesus could have forced the point. He could have tried to make him say it.

But He didn't. He let it go.

Instead, seeing the lawyer got the right answer, He pressed hard and commanded him, "Go and do the same." It's like He said, "If you'd just let God's mercy reign in your heart, you'd know what the Samaritan knew. You'd do what the Samaritan did, and you'd be changed forever. But instead, you're just like your colleagues—the priest, the Levite. Don't be. Go, be like the Samaritan. Love your neighbor. Bring the kingdom of God to everyone you meet. No matter who they are. Can you do that? Will you do that?"

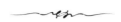

It was the perfect storm.

Some ten days before my chaplaincy program ended, Sam was diagnosed with an upper respiratory infection. This served to exacerbate his coughing problem—which was louder that week, the spasms longer and more frequent.

As much as he tried to control it, he couldn't.

It scared him even more. He'd cry for help, but all he'd get in return was an even stronger reaction from his ward mates. They didn't want him around. He tried to find privacy, but there was nowhere to go. Not on this ward. Somebody was always somewhere. And everybody just kept pushing him away.

Day after day, it only seemed to worsen. In between his coughing spells, Sam's mood was downcast, withdrawn. He just wasn't himself.

Then, finally, it all erupted.

He'd wandered into the game room. Over half the people were there. No aides or nurses or doctors. The TV was blasting, and Sam wasn't even coughing. Just the sight of him, that's all, and they rose up. As if it was all planned. They began yelling at him. Pushing him. Forcing him to the corner of the room where, when he hit the wall, he slumped down, covering his head with his hands.

That's when I got there. They were kicking him. Slapping him. All of it triggered the coughing again. Louder than before. Frenzied and panicked. Within seconds, the aides and staff rushed in, breaking it up. Sam got up from the floor and ran out of the room as fast as he could, crying and coughing hysterically. I followed him, knowing he'd head for the glassed-in porch.

Which is exactly what he did.

The few people there, the moment they saw Sam, left the room. He threw himself onto the couch, buried his head in his hands, and cried—and coughed—and cried more.

I pulled up a chair. It was my turn now.

I'd spent most of the summer watching Sam love his ward mates with a passion and freedom I'd never imagined. Somehow, for Sam, it was always about them—not him. It was as if the Lord had assigned him as a guardian angel to this ward with one simple assignment: "Sam, go love them. Each one, with all you've got. And I will be with you."

And Sam did. Sometimes with words. Sometimes not. Never with a plan or an agenda or some ulterior motive. With no care for how he was treated yesterday. Or last week. Or whenever. Just today, doing what he knew to do. But this day, of all days, was the worst. It was the first time a gang had risen up like that and yelled, beaten, and hurt him. I could see his heart was crushed.

It was my turn to be Sam to Sam.

And what would he do first? He'd get tissues. And that's what I did.

A nurse came in to check on Sam. She spent a few minutes examining him, checking if anything was broken and for any cuts or bleeding. She tried to calm him down. I think he tried too—but it was all too much for him. His breathing became rapid. He started hyperventilating.

The nurse then began to speak calmly to him. She did it well. It took a few minutes, but he slowly responded. His coughing spasms started subsiding. The nurse stayed until Sam settled, but the moment she rose to leave, the coughing came back. She promised she'd return in a little while.

Sam nodded but started crying again.

I pulled my chair closer.

No words. No tools to try to fix things.

As expected, no one from the ward came to see how he was doing—as he would have done with them. Not one person. I wondered if Sam knew.

He did.

"Nobody's here. Nobody loves me," he said through his cries. He told me he wanted to see his brother. He wanted to leave this godforsaken place. He wanted to go home and never come back.

I wondered if he had a home. I stayed next to him, just like he taught me.

For a while, he was calm again. But the moment the coughing came back, the fears did too. He looked at the door. He was afraid all his ward mates were going to come rushing through it and attack him again. He buried his head into the side of the couch—hoping to muffle the sound. I put my hand on his arm.

Like I'd seen him do with others crying.

And I saw him like I didn't want to see him. He was, for me, right then, the beaten man in the gospel story—half dead—lying on the side of the road. But for him, there was no Samaritan. No one who would come, pick up his broken body, and take him to where he could be healed from this wretched disease.

So he could feel human again.

I thought about the poor man, Lazarus, Jesus talked about. Sitting outside the rich man's house. No food. No scraps. Dogs licking his wounds. Left alone to die with no Samaritan ever coming to his rescue.

Not until he breathed his last. Then, the angels came (see Luke 16:20–22).

Would this be Sam's story? Would he die here on the ward? By himself? Coughing, crying, scared, alone?

"Jesus was rejected too, you know," he said, surprising me. "Nobody cared. Nobody came. Not for Him. Not for me. I just want to go home."

I sat there wishing I could be there when it happened. When the angels came. When the doors of the eternal kingdom of our Lord and Savior, Jesus Christ, opened wide and Sam finally beheld the face of the Great Samaritan himself. But I knew I wouldn't be. I'd be leaving soon. The summer was almost over. And just the thought of leaving him like this made me—like him—cry.

QUESTIONS FOR REFLECTION

The world needs more than us believing in God's mercy. They need to see us live His mercy. What needs to change in us? In our churches?

Where are the people in your community (and the world) like Sam—suffering, scared, and alone? If we are to "Go and do the same," how and when will you go and do it?

36

BLACKOUT

―✧―

Reflections on Luke 10:38

*Now as they were traveling along, He entered a village;
and a woman named Martha welcomed Him into her home.*

—LUKE 10:38

Why is the lawyer gone?

What happened to him? One minute we're standing with Jesus. He was telling the lawyer to go do what the Samaritan did: Go live mercy! Go love God with all your heart so you can love your neighbor with all your heart.

The next minute, the legal expert was gone.

But why? This is the key moment of the conversation. We need to know how he responded to Jesus. Did he get it? Did he understand he was not allowed to pick and choose his "neighbor"? We're to love the stranger. We're to love the Samaritans. We're to love anybody and everybody no matter if we think they're nobodies.

But we get nothing. No nod of the head. No sign he agreed.

The scene blacks out and the next scene pops up: Jesus was traveling with His disciples toward Martha's home. The lawyer had vanished from the stage forever. We can't trace him in other gospel accounts. We don't know his name. We have no way of resolving the question of what happened to this man's soul.

Are we to assume everything turned out well?

It did for the man unjustly beaten. The Samaritan brought him back to health. Are we to assume our Lord did the same for the brilliant lawyer? If so, did he go back to his colleagues and align himself with people like Joseph of Arimathea and Nicodemus? Did he stand in defense of Jesus at His trial?

Or, maybe not. Maybe he left the conversation with Jesus and didn't know how to process it all. Then, after Jesus was raised, he joined his colleagues as "a great many of the priests were becoming obedient to the faith" (Acts 6:7). Was that his story? Did it turn out well for him?

Or did he leave Jesus with his heart hardened all the more?

Or worse, did he join the political forces that seized Jesus and put Him to violent death? Was there no Damascus Road conversion in his life?

Why don't we know?

There are too many Bible stories like this. What happened to the Prodigal Son's brother? Did the rich man who walked away from Jesus walk away forever? What about our Lord's disciples who left Him (see John 6:66)? Did some come back? And what about Demas, who served with the apostle Paul and then left, "having loved this present world" more (see 2 Tim. 4:10)? Was it a phase? Did he come back?

Why this uncomfortable world of uncertainty?

And what does it mean for us? Why can't everything in life be neatly resolved? Why can't all our questions find clear, simple answers?

But that's not the Lord's design. Not here in this life. Often, we have to live with mysteries and ambiguities.

But one thing is certain: Mercy is here. Mercy has come. It is ours to receive.

Before—way before—the blackout comes.

I stayed with Sam that day until he finally walked off. I didn't follow him this time. Instead, I got out the little notebook in my back pocket and wrote down some of our conversation. He'd said some things I never wanted to forget.

"God doesn't look down on anyone," he told me. And, "Jesus is my only friend. He's all I've got."[1]

He was skittish the next few days, doing his best to stay away from everybody. His respiratory infection passed and, with it, thankfully, the memory of his ward mates turning on him. Sam was Sam again, doing everything he could to make everyone around him feel cared for and loved.

On the day before the program ended, I had my final meeting with Leslie.

"I think your bishop is going to be pleased," he assured me. "You worked hard this summer, and I think you achieved what he had in mind for you."

"That is not fair!" I teased.

"Why not?"

"Because I'm not supposed to care about the bishop's reaction! You helped me see that. You put my focus where it should've been—with the people and staff on my ward. You tried to throw me out of this program! Remember?"

"Yes, I do!" Leslie said, laughing.

"I can't thank you enough for that. I was pretty angry when I got here."

"So you're glad you stayed?"

"Yeah, and I want to ask a favor. I want to come back this fall, maybe a couple of Saturdays during visiting hours, and check on Sam. Is that OK?"

"No," he said quickly, firmly.

"There's a two-hour window where family and friends visit. I asked Sam's doctor if it would be all right, and she seemed to think it'd be fine."

"The answer is no," Leslie stated again. "When you leave, you leave. It's over."

"What if I did it with you? Maybe came on a weekday. I could go to the ward for a little while, spend time with everybody, and then report back to you after it's over. Maybe once a month. I really want to keep coming back."

He didn't respond this time.

"Why not?" I asked.

"Why are you doing this? For you or for Sam?"

I didn't have an answer for that.

"Tomorrow you'll go to the ward for the last time," he instructed. "Afterward, you'll hand me the key to the ward, and that's it. Is that clear?"

I nodded, but tried again.

"Could I call you once in a while and see how Sam is doing? The doctor told me she doesn't think he has much time left. I'd like to know how he's doing."

He smiled gently, and I thought for just a second he'd say yes. He didn't. He told me again I had one more time with Sam and that would be it. As he explained his reasons, I realized the same was true with him. This was our last time together, and he, like Sam, had profoundly impacted my life. In different ways, they both had been a gift from God.

They knew how to love others—Jesus' way.

As he prayed for me, a deep sadness seized my heart. I didn't want to leave him or Sam or this hospital. But I had to.

It was time to say good-bye.

And so, the next day, I went on the ward for the last time. It didn't surprise me to find Sam sitting next to a guy who'd kicked him the week before. For whatever reason, the guy was crying, and Sam had a box of tissues in hand, sitting close, his hand resting on his back. Sam looked peaceful, not scared.

A little while later, he saw me.

"You're leaving today," he announced.

"Yeah," I said, amazed he remembered. I was never sure if Sam even knew my name. He grabbed my hand and slowly paraded me through the ward. He wanted me to spend time with everybody. A proper good-bye. Not just with a few, but with all of them. It's like he knew all along I was tasked to love the thirty equally. Something Sam did every day of his life.

Truth be told, I didn't. I loved Sam more.

It came time to leave. Sam and I parted abruptly. He smiled and said what he said when he first met me: "You're going to be all right!" He patted my hand and walked off, heading for the game room. He looked happy. Still coughing. And I was left with no sense that tomorrow, a month from tomorrow, a year from tomorrow, he'd remember me.

But I'd remember him and always have.

Soon after, I left the ward and closed the door behind me. Like the ending of some movies, everything blacked out and Sam disappeared into time.

That was twenty-nine years ago. I often wonder what happened to him. And every time I do, I reach the same conclusion. I think about what he taught me. For he was, to me, like the Samaritan of old. He showed me—in practical and real ways—how to live the second Great Commandment. So I could be like Sam. So I could do what Jesus said the lawyer should do: "Go and do likewise."

Or to say it as I saw Sam live it: "Show mercy. Then after that, show mercy—no matter how they react, no matter how it feels. And when you're done showing mercy, do it again. And again. Till you reach always and forever."

QUESTIONS FOR REFLECTION

Do you know people in blackout? They've heard the gospel of mercy but it's a mystery. Are they changed? Are they saved? When has this been you?

What if we asked the Holy Spirit to empower us—and our church—to show mercy like Sam? And after that, show mercy again and always?

NOTE

1. Thaddeus Barnum, *Real Love: Where Bible and Life Meet* (Indianapolis: Wesleyan Publishing House, 2014), 230.

PART 6

A SERVANT AND HIS TOWEL

37

FILLED WITH ATTITUDE

Reflections on John 13:1–4

Jesus, knowing that the Father had given all things into His hands, and that He had come forth from God and was going back to God, got up from supper, and laid aside His garments.

—JOHN 13:3–4

God often speaks His story in simple earthly pictures.

A rainbow in the sky. The circumcising of an infant boy on his eighth day. A mark of blood on a doorpost. A heap of twelve stones taken from the dry riverbed of the Jordan. A loaf of bread in the hands of our Savior lifted to His Father for blessing. Then He broke it and gave it. A simple act. A common act.

And by it, He told His story. He said, "I am the bread of life." He said, "If anyone eats of this bread, he will live forever" (John 6:35, 51).

Again, "Take, eat; this is My body" (Matt. 26:26).

For as He breaks the bread, we glimpse His own breaking on the cross. And as He gives the bread, we see His invitation to freely receive His gift of eternal life.

So it was, on the night before He died, He did it again. He spoke. Not, at first, with words. But through a simple act. A common act. And by doing it, He explained the heart of God. He explained why He was about to suffer. And, with utmost simplicity, He told us to do with each other, with everyone, what He was about to do.

It was time.

Soon enough, He'd be back with His Father. He'd come from Him. He'd go back to Him. No matter how it appeared to others, He knew His Father had given "all things" into His hands. Did the Devil know that? Or did he think he was stronger, more powerful than Jesus? He'd already made his first move. He'd won Judas's heart. In a few hours, he'd muster all the powers of darkness against our Lord.

It was time. One simple act to show His love.

Why hadn't it been done yet? It should've happened the moment they arrived. At the very latest, before they'd reclined at the table for the Passover meal. Why was no servant around? Who'd failed to make proper preparations? Did anyone notice or say something? Why didn't one of the Twelve offer to do it?

Our Lord stopped eating His supper.

He got up from the table and began to disrobe. One garment. Then the next. Until He stood in front of the Twelve wearing only a loincloth.

Dressed as a poor, common slave.[1]

An apostle would later capture this image in words: He "took upon him the form of a servant." He "made himself of no reputation" (Phil. 2:7 KJV).

For the most part, the apostle was speaking about our Lord's incarnation. Before time began, Jesus decided with His Father, and with the Holy Spirit, to disrobe himself of His glory and become man. This is the news of Bethlehem: A child is born— fully God, fully man—who willingly took "the form of a servant."

But the apostle also spoke of this moment. This is the news of the final Passover: Our Lord has come to serve and not be served. And if He did this, we are to do the same. "Have this atti- tude in yourselves," urged the apostle (Phil. 2:5; see Mark 10:45).

For there He stands, God the Son, dressed in a loincloth.

A poor, common slave.

I first met John in the fall of 1988.

Erilynne and I were pastoring a church just outside Pittsburgh. It was a young church, only a few years old. By late October, we'd finished our first building project and moved out of our rented space and into our new church home.

John first visited on a Sunday morning in September. Soon after, he came every week. I knew three things about him: He was an Anglican priest from Africa, he'd been granted a two-year scholarship to study at a local seminary, and he was alone. "There were no extra monies to bring my wife and five children to America," he told me, and I could see the pain on his face.

"We need to get together soon," I promised him.

But I never followed through. I was too busy with the building project and the daily care of the church. Finally, in early December, I asked if he'd help out at the Sunday service and then have lunch afterward. He readily agreed.

But to be honest, I had no idea of my arrogance.

I actually thought we'd go out to lunch and he'd tell us how we could help him. He was a poor African clergyman, alone in America, without his family. No doubt, he had a long list of needs. Surely we could do something to help.

What's wrong with that?

It never occurred to me I was the one in need. Not him.

"What part of Africa do you come from?" I asked before the Sunday service.

"Rwanda," he said, his accent thick. "But since the civil war of 1959, we've been exiled to Uganda."[2]

I immediately asked him about Idi Amin, the infamous president of Uganda in the 1970s who brutally terrorized the country.

"I have seen that evil man face-to-face as he danced in our streets as a madman, his machine guns on either hip. I was no more than two feet from him." He paused, looking straight at me. "I also know his soldiers. They have had their guns at my head, jammed against my temple."

"What?"

"They came looking for my bishop. I was the vicar of St. Peter's Cathedral in Hoima town. I was sitting in my office when the soldiers banged on the door and told me at gunpoint that I was going to die because my bishop had escaped the country. I told them straightaway that my bishop was sitting in his office that very moment. When they heard this, they told me that if he was there, I would live. If not, I would die. They dragged me to his office with their guns pressing into my head."

"And?"

"By God's grace, he was sitting at his desk, just as I told them."

Then the stories only got worse. He shared that government soldiers would randomly kill people. As he and other clergy tried to care for the dead bodies—to give them proper burial—the soldiers shot at them too.

"It was a very scary time," he said. "We never knew what they would do next. Nobody was safe. Everybody lost somebody they loved. The number of widows and orphans was just too much. Even now, the country hasn't recovered."

It was almost time for the service to begin.

I asked John if he'd mind sharing some of his story with the congregation. "Tell us what it was like to be a Christian under Idi Amin's rule."

He kindly agreed.

Some in the congregation didn't understand him because of his accent. But many of us did. He described how he came to saving faith in Jesus Christ as a young man and how he entered His service. "The Lord told me people need to hear about Jesus. They need to have their names in the Book of Life."

He told us he was no stranger to poverty—life without a constant flow of electricity, clean water, access to health care professionals, or medicine, transportation to town, or a solid metal roof overhead to protect his family from seasonal rains.

And then he talked about the killings, the military oppression, the sleepless nights when gunfire shattered the quiet and screams echoed through mountains and valleys. He talked about facing death—more than once—simply for confessing Jesus as his Lord to his extremist Muslim captors.

There was no heroism in his voice.

"We give all glory to God," he exclaimed. "He alone gives us the strength we need to face the evil powers."

He prayed for us and then sat down.

I tried to take it all in. Here I am, a clergyman from an affluent and peaceful land where being a Christian requires little risk, low cost, and almost no sacrifice. And there he is, with a tested faith that towers over mine. He knows the sufferings in this world—and about suffering for Christ—in ways I've never known. Who was I to help him?

At lunch, he surprised me. At one point during the meal, a big smile lit his face. "I've been asking the Lord," he said, his words filled with a gentle, humble attitude.

"What's that?" I asked back.

"How I can help you while I'm here."

I wanted to respond, "I'm supposed to ask you that!" But I didn't. He was right. Our roles had reversed. He had far more to give me than I had to give him.

QUESTIONS FOR REFLECTION

What does the picture of our Lord dressed as a common slave tell you about the heart of God? About His mercy to you? About His love for you?

Consider 2 Corinthians 8:9 and James 2:5. If we are filled with the attitude of our Lord, how can we ever look down on the poor? On anyone?

NOTES

1. Leon Morris wrote, "Jesus stripped to a loin cloth, just like a slave" (*The Gospel according to John* [Grand Rapids, MI: Eerdmans, 1971], 615, note 15.

2. Thaddeus Barnum, *Never Silent: How Third World Missionaries Are Bringing the Gospel to the US* (Colorado Springs: Eleison, 2008), 25–29.

38

DRESSED IN A TOWEL

Reflections on John 13:3–5

Jesus . . . got up from supper, and laid aside
His garments; and taking a towel, He girded Himself.
Then He poured water into the basin.

—JOHN 13:3–5

Jesus did what should never be done.

He broke our rules. We have a fixed social order. We have class distinctions. Those below us work to be like us. Those above us never stoop to come down to us. There are rules. There are ancient boundaries society demands we honor.

Every society. And that night was no different.

Jewish men never touched that towel. Not even Jewish men who were slaves. Women could. Children could. But it was generally reserved for the lowest class of people. Gentile slaves. Mere property. Society's worst. Barely recognized as human.[1]

Nobody who was anybody touched that towel.

And yet, He did.

Did the Twelve stop eating, stop talking? Were their eyes fixed on Him? Why didn't one of them stop Him? Or help Him? Or tell Him he'd do it instead? But it seemed no one moved. They watched Him take the towel and open it up. They knew exactly what He was doing. He was not just looking like a slave.

He was about to do what slaves did.

The servant towel was long. It was designed first to be worn: then, with the extra material out front, to dry the washed feet.[2] And that's exactly what Jesus did. He wrapped the towel around His waist. It was the first step. Then He reached for the basin. It was all there. Everything needed for washing. Just no servant. But now, the Servant was here. He reached for the jug of water.

He poured. It was, perhaps, the only sound in the upper room.

Why was He doing this? If anything, they should have been washing His feet. How many times over the previous three and a half years had they seen people fall at His feet? Who could forget the woman who washed His feet with her tears and dried them with her hair? They should have been doing this to Him, not the other way around.

It had never been done before. Not in Jewish custom. Not like this. No doubt no one moved. Most likely, no one could, even if they tried.

He put the jug down, grabbed the basin, turned to them, and stood there, dressed in a servant's towel, holding the basin of water with both hands. He decided where to start, took a step, then another, and quietly moved toward them.

During John's two years in the States, we worked on projects together. The first, most important, was to bring Harriet, his wife, and their two youngest children, Joy and Andrew, to be with John for his last year of study.

Some calls, a few generous donors, and our prayers were answered.

The second project was more complicated. John and I had many long talks about ways we could serve the poor in his home community. Together, we dreamed of shipping a large container to Uganda full of medical supplies, clothing, fabric, furniture, seed, tools, schoolbooks, toys, art supplies, bicycles, appliances, various household items, and, if possible, a car.

John needed a car. In his role as an Anglican archdeacon, he traveled great distances from church to church on his bicycle—his only means of transport.

We drafted a budget.

Along with the mission committee at church, I put together a brochure designed to reach suppliers who'd donate goods and benefactors who'd give money.

I showed it to John.

"Here's the plan," I suggested. "We know pastors all across the country who'll invite you to preach in their church. We'll make sure they pass this brochure out and raise money for the project."

"No," John said sternly.

"But John, we have to."

"No!" he repeated. "I will preach the gospel. I will not raise funds."

"Fair enough. We can ask the pastors to do it."

He shook his head. "No mixing. If I hold the Bible in one hand and tell people about Jesus, but with the other hand I hold out for money, who will believe what I say about Jesus? All they will see is a poor African asking for money. No, I'll preach the gospel. Full stop! Nothing more!"

"We'll never raise the funds that way, John."

"It's not true. This project is the Lord's project. It is for the poor in my country. The Lord will do this for His glory, not ours. You must have faith."

"So, you won't even take the brochures with you?" I asked, almost pleading.

Again, he shook his head, and it reminded me of the time John was being interviewed at a wealthy church in downtown Pittsburgh. A man stood up, wanting to make a donation, and asked, "What can I do for you?"

John replied quickly, "You can be in relationship with me and my family. You know, when we come to the cross of Jesus, we all stand on level ground."

The man looked puzzled. I don't think he understood.

That moment gave me insight into John. He was not first a poor African man. He was not someone to look down on, deserving our pity and begging for our charity. He was first a Christian man, a sinner saved by grace, one for whom Christ died and rose again. This is where it all starts—at the cross.

On level ground.

The rich, the educated, the powerful, the influential, the noble, and the elite have no stature over the poor, the under-educated, and the so-called primitive people by some in the First World. Not at the cross. Here, John taught me, we all stand together. Nobody above the other. Nobody under. Each helping each.

Soon enough, John began his travels, preaching in churches across the country. One weekend, John came back with a check for five thousand dollars for the shipment.

"Did you tell them about the project?" I asked, elated.

"No!" he said, with a smle on his face. "People's hearts were moved by the Lord, and they gave spontaneously. My brother, I told you this was going to happen. The Lord is taking care of this project. He will do it!" And He did. We actually received more than we needed—both in supplies and donations—weeks ahead of schedule. I'd never seen anything like it before.

John's strong faith kept strengthening my weak faith.

Eventually time passed and John and Harriet moved back to Uganda.

Each year, we raised enough funds to bring John back to the States. He'd travel the country, preaching Jesus, with more invitations than his time allowed. And every year, I saw a growing burden weighing on his soul.

"It's the children," he'd tell me. "AIDS is killing our people. Parents are dying, and where do their kids go?"

He wanted to start an orphanage.

In the early 1990s, an exploratory team from three US churches flew to Uganda and began gathering facts, assessing costs, and developing strategies. John had already found a rental facility as well as a woman skilled both in nursing and administration to run the home.

Stateside, we wrote grant proposals. We called on pastors who knew John to pray.

I shouldn't have been surprised, but I was. Money started pouring in. People who knew John, who loved and trusted John, suddenly jumped on board wanting to sponsor a child. The vision had sprouted wings and started to fly.

In January 1994, Erilynne and I got to see it firsthand.

It was our first trip to Africa. On our second day there, John and Harriet took us to see the facility. The home—now called the Blessed Mustard Seed Babies Home—would not officially open until July 1, 1994. But even in the midst of construction, babies and staff already lived there.[3]

And there stood John. I will never forget that day.

He held a baby in his arms. The child was orphaned and only a few months old. "You know, when we do this," John said, his eyes bright, a smile stretched across his face, "we love Jesus! Just like He said, 'Whoever receives one such child in My name receives Me.'"

And somehow, under the African sun, it all made sense.

As Jesus came to love us, we do the same for others. And every time we do, we love Him back—over and over again.

All these years later, the Blessed Mustard Seed Babies Home is still going strong. A new generation of children now lives there. And I can still hear John's voice as he held that beautiful little girl, now in her twenties: "When we do this, we love Jesus!"

QUESTIONS FOR REFLECTION

When have you wrestled with pride? Are there tasks you'd never consider doing? What does it mean to you that our Lord is wearing this towel?

What does the expression "level ground" mean to you? Do you think John is right: When we love others as Jesus has loved us, we are loving Him?

NOTES

1. George R. Beasley-Murray, *John*, Word Biblical Commentary, vol. 6 (Dallas: Word, 1987), 233.

2. Leon Morris, *The Gospel according to John* (Grand Rapids, MI: Eerdmans, 1971), 616.

3. Thaddeus Barnum, *Never Silent: How Third World Missionaries Are Bringing the Gospel to the US* (Colorado Springs: Eleison, 2008), 32–35. For more information on the Blessed Mustard Seed Babies Home, go to www.mustardseedproject.org.

39

UPS AND DOWNS

Reflections on John 13:4–5

*He poured water into the basin, and began
to wash the disciples' feet.*

—JOHN 13:5

He poured. He began to wash. And in between, He moved.

First, moving toward them. Then reaching down, carefully setting the basin on the floor. Then getting down himself. Perhaps on His knees. He readied the towel. And then, with His hands, He touched their feet and began.

When slaves do it, who notices? Does it even interrupt the conversation?

But what happens when God does it?

This motion—the motion down—is His story. Every bit of it. It is the priceless jewel of the "good news" of the gospel. Our Lord moves down.

Down from His eternal glory and into a virgin's womb. Down from the royal majesty due Him as the promised Son of King David whose "kingdom will have no end." Down into a common life as a child in Nazareth and into poverty, where all his mother and father could afford at His birth was a sacrificial offering of turtledoves and pigeons.

"He took the form of a servant" (see Luke 1:33; 2:22–24).

And now, at the last Passover meal, He stepped down again. He became a slave. He willingly took the lowest of all positions. But this wasn't it. He wasn't done. It was only a foreshadowing— a physical picture—of what He would do the next day. Soon enough, the cross beam would stretch across His back. He would be crucified in a way only the worst and the most wicked die. And He would go down again.

Down into death. Down into the fiery baptism of God's judgment against all sin, for all time. Down to depths infinite and inconceivable.

This motion down. It's His story. This is our God.

It's not the Devil's story. From his beginnings, this angelic creature lusted for "up." He said in his heart, "I will ascend to heaven. . . . I will make myself like the Most High" (Isa. 14:13–14; see also Ezek. 28:14–17). In his reign over the fallen human race, this motion remains his motion.

His kingdom is the up kingdom. Everybody wants up. Greater position and title. Greater recognition, praise, honor, and adoration, and a name that lasts forever.

No one wants down. No one chooses down.

The Devil's lust for up is insatiable. When faced with Jesus, he wanted more than his feet washed. He wanted the Son of God to worship him. For him, nothing is greater or higher than that— to be exalted and worshiped by God himself (see Matt. 4:8–10).

This is the Devil's heart. This is the engine that drives this present age.

Everything is up. Always up.

But it is not the kingdom of God. Nor the heart of God. And when our Lord came to us, He taught us this: The way up is the way down. If we want to be great, we serve. If we want to be first, we must be last. For the exalted are humbled, and the humbled are exalted. And He didn't just teach it. He did it. He chose down.

It's how He moves. It's how those who love Him move too.

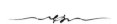

When John came to the States in September 1994, he was a different man.

A month prior, he'd entered his native country of Rwanda for the first time in thirty-five years. He'd been exiled with his family in 1959 at age fourteen. The Hutu ethnic group had come into power and waged war against the Tutsi ethnic group. The violence was extreme in the northwest where John was born and raised. His family was Tutsi. They had no choice but to flee the country.

By April 1994, the Hutu government enforced the complete genocide of the Tutsi people. For the next one hundred days, nearly a million people were slaughtered.

"There are no devils left in hell," a missionary told reporters a few weeks into the bloodshed. "They are all in Rwanda."[1]

Within a few weeks after the war ended, John led an expedition of nine clergymen to tour the remains of his country.

"It was beyond the scope of what the human mind can take in," John told us that fall. "We thought—no human being could do this to another human being. We saw mass graves containing more than twenty-five thousand dead bodies. . . . It was a terrible shock—real trauma. We were all in tears."

He interviewed people in their homes, in churches, and in medical clinics.

"We had to see the brokenness of our country. . . . In my heart, I knew God was calling me to be part of the healing and reconciliation of my people. . . . I knew beyond any doubt that the Lord was bigger than their brokenness. He is the only one who can bring about real and lasting transformation."

And so, John spent the next few years traveling back and forth from Uganda to Rwanda. In the spring of 1997, he was elected to the office of Anglican bishop in the northwest. Nothing could have scared me more.

The northwest of Rwanda was not stable.

John's friend told us, "There are retribution killings going on day and night. Rebel forces are crossing Zaire's border into Rwanda." Tutsis were still being killed. And then he said an ambush had been set against John's life.

I wrote John, concerned and anxious.

He wrote back and said, "The ambush, which we survived, was not intended to hurt me in particular. It was a general ambush which took place before my election." Then he wrote of an attack on a girls' high school. The killers tried to separate the Hutu girls from the Tutsi girls—but the students refused. They bound themselves together as one. The killers shot randomly, killing eighteen.

"I am telling you," John wrote, "we shall never forget these brave girls."

I feared for John's life. The capital city of Kigali was an hour and a half away. Kigali was secure. The northwest—for a Tutsi, and a prominent Tutsi bishop—was not. And so I did what I thought was right. I wrote. I called. I begged for John not to live in the northwest. "Live in Kigali and commute until the killings subside," I pleaded.

John responded by sending a fax on May 12, 1997, that read, "We hope to have a hired house in Ruhengeri town (in the northwest). Pray continually for our protection. We are bound to serve Jesus in all places."

But on the phone, I could tell he was upset with me. "Why would we do that? Are we supposed to protect ourselves first—then serve? No! If they are suffering, we suffer too."

I tried to argue. "But you won't be able to serve if the rebels kill you."

He didn't budge. He kept saying, "You should know these things. Did Jesus avoid the cross to keep himself safe? Why should we?" He said it again and again: "God is clear in His call to us. We are moving to Ruhengeri."

Meanwhile, back in the States, we kept hearing of more rebel activity in the northwest. More ambushes, more fighting, more killings.

Over the next year, it got worse. John sent continual reports:

Yesterday, many people were killed on one of the university campuses in Mudende: 144 perished at the hand of infiltrators . . . many other people died. Hence, we have over 200 refugees at one of our churches in the area. We are in crisis. We need you to pray because we are faced with the practical problem of feeding these people and giving them shelter.

We lost five people at the hands of infiltrators . . . killing the principal of our high school, a lady who worked for the school, and her two teenagers (who are related to me).

We lost one of our pastors, who left a widow and seven orphans.

By midsummer 1998, John lamented, "Three of my clergy and many lay pastors were killed along with their families. Many of our dear Christians also died in the violent attacks of my first year."

And for John, there were too many close calls:

I could see . . . infiltrators. I told the priest driving the car to speed up. We were able to drive past them before they got settled. The van behind us got intercepted. Five people were killed.

But that's the difference between John and me.

I would've lived in Kigali, protected my family, and commuted to work. Not John. He knew Jesus' way. For Jesus doesn't move up. He moves down. Not just by being with His people in their suffering. But serving them there.

On hands and knees. With a towel, basin, and some water.

I saw this principle alive in John and Harriet. Even at the risk of their own lives. And I knew then what I know now: I don't know how to choose "down" like that—not when it puts me as risk.

QUESTIONS FOR REFLECTION

Do you choose up or down? How has up shaped your identity? What does down teach you about our Lord? About His cross? About you?

How do you answer John's questions: Are we supposed to protect ourselves first—then serve? Did Jesus avoid the cross to keep himself safe—why should we?

NOTE

1. Thaddeus Barnum, *Never Silent: How Third World Missionaries Are Bringing the Gospel to the US* (Colorado Springs: Eleison, 2008), 48–69.

40

THE SAVIOR'S LOVE

Reflections on John 13:3–5, 12

Jesus . . . began to wash the disciples' feet and to wipe them with the towel with which He was girded . . . . So when He had washed their feet . . .

—JOHN 13:3–5, 12

Whose feet were first?

John only recorded the conversation between Jesus and Peter. But did the disciples all talk to Him? Did they all, like Peter, try to stop Him? Was Peter first? Or maybe Philip, Bartholomew, or Thomas?

And how long did it take? He was the only foot washer that night. For each one. Around the table. So how did He do it? When He finished with one, did He pick up the basin and move on His knees to the next one? Or did He stand up each time? How long did He spend with each person? More than usual?

Andrew, James, John.

Did He have to get up from time to time, empty the dirty water, clean the basin, and fill it with fresh water again? Did He have to change towels? How often? And was there any sound in the upper room but Him? Who could eat? Who could talk while their Lord, their Teacher, washed their feet? Was He quiet? Did He speak out their names when He came to them?

Matthew, James, Thaddaeus, Simon.

He didn't wash the feet of a few. He washed them all.

At some point, He came to Judas. Was he first? Was he somewhere in the middle? No matter—He did not single Judas out. What He did for the others, He did for Judas, gently taking his feet and washing them. Even though Jesus already knew Satan had come to him. He'd "put it into the heart of Judas" to betray Him (John 13:2). And before supper's end, it would happen. The unimaginable.

Satan "entered into" Judas (13:27).

Isn't it obvious? The Eleven had no clue. They had no idea who Jesus was talking about when, after the washing, He announced, "One of you will betray me." Again, "You are clean, but not all of you." This can mean only one thing. Our Lord treated Judas as He did the others. He washed, He loved, He cared—each one the same.

How is that possible? How can anyone wash their betrayer's feet?

But He did.

And this one moment is forever fixed in time. It is remembered by all who know the Savior's love. For there He is, kneeling in front of Judas, holding his feet in His hands and washing. Spending just as much time. Giving just as much love.

We never forget.

And we do the same. We wash feet. All feet. It doesn't matter whose they are. What they've done. What they will do. How they've hurt us. How they will hurt us. We wash as He washed. We love as He loves. We show no partiality, ever.

For we are a people who never forget.

On June 8, 1997, John was consecrated bishop in front of twenty-five hundred people. It was a day of quiet, unspoken miracle. In the land of the northwest, dominated by Hutus, the Lord had called a Tutsi to lead His church.

But how was John to do it?

Too many people were homeless. Too many widows, orphans, men roaming the streets without work, and families locked in their homes afraid to work in the fields for fear of being killed by infiltrators. People needed food, clothing, medical treatment, education, vocational training, post-trauma counseling, and a tiny flicker of hope that peace and stability were possible.[1]

Where was he to start?

Making it worse, the church had lost its standing in the nation. There were too many stories of church officials, bishops, and pastors—across denominations—who openly supported the Hutu government. Some of these church leaders, the world later learned, actually participated in the genocide.

The church had become unsafe.

John had to make it safe again. How else would his nation recover? Where would it find the power to heal, forgive, and reconcile if not in the death and resurrection of the Lord Jesus Christ? Something had to change.

John had to do—had to *be*—different.

He traveled the northwest. He met with the clergy, preached in the churches, and assessed the people's needs. Nothing concerned him more than the vast population of orphans. He knew that even before the genocide, roughly 60 percent of the Rwandan population was illiterate.

To effect lasting change, these orphans needed schools. The best schools with the best teachers and curriculum.

He dreamed big. He wanted one of these schools, the Sonrise School, to be one of the best in the country.[2] He wanted it to produce a new generation of leaders who'd lead Rwanda into the future. And in the hearts of those leaders, they'd know Jesus Christ as their Lord.

John was off to a good start. Until news came.

A few months after John was made bishop, his niece came for a visit. Her name was Madu. She was a sixteen-year-old high school student, about the same age as John and Harriet's own daughters. She'd often come to visit. She and her cousins were close friends. Her visits always brought the family joy.

But this particular time, she was scared.

She told John that she and her mother, her sister and brother, were afraid of the infiltrators. Ethnically, they were a mixed family. Her father was a Tutsi, her mother a Hutu. She feared the rebels had already targeted them. She wanted to know if her family could come and stay with John and Harriet. They lived in another town. Perhaps they could find a house nearby?

John later told me, "I reassured her that the provisions for the move were cared for and that they should come immediately."

Madu went back home and prepared to move.

But that same night, the rebels came.

John's description of that night was graphic and horrifying. The infiltrators didn't just kill Madu. They tortured her. They raped her. They let her feel the machetes slowly dismember her.

"We could not conceive," John said to me, "none of us could, the pain this dear girl went through. To this day, we deeply grieve her loss."

And not just her death. They killed her mother, brother, and sister.

"Early the next morning," John reported, "some of the Christians from that town came out of hiding and brought us the news. We had to make burial arrangements, but the soldiers would not let me attend my family's burial. They told me, as a bishop coming to this town, I would attract public attention and many more people would die."

John and his family were left to mourn in silence.

The war was not over. Everybody said it ended in the summer of 1994. But it had not. Three years later, in the northwest, the war raged on.

Countrymen killing their own countrymen.

The next spring, Erilynne and I visited John and Harriet in Rwanda. The grief was still palpable—as if Madu and her family had died only weeks before.

"It was a tragic and devastating moment in our lives," they shared with us. "It was very painful for our children."

It shook them, shook them deep.

They were Tutsis in a Hutu world. Their job was to preach Jesus because they knew that by His cross, forgiveness was possible. By His resurrection, reconciliation was possible. The Rwandan people could hear the message of reconciliation from secular leaders. But they needed more than the message. They needed its power, and that power comes from Jesus Christ.

Power to comfort, heal, and cleanse the soul.

But how could they do it now?

John and Harriet were suffering. Every time they traveled the northwest, the rebels—the infiltrators—could be anywhere, intermingled in the crowds. Maybe the same people who'd killed their family. And if they were nearby, could they forgive them? How does that happen? How does the Savior's love work? How do we love the people who've violently trampled and violated our souls? How do we do what our Savior did?

And kneel down to carefully, compassionately wash even their feet?

QUESTIONS FOR REFLECTION

Can you, trusting in Jesus, love as He loves—showing mercy without partiality, able to wash all feet? How would the church be different if we lived as people who "never forget"?

How does the Savior's love work practically? How can John wash the feet of those who killed his family? How can you for those who have hurt you?

NOTES

1. Thaddeus Barnum, *Never Silent: How Third World Missionaries Are Bringing the Gospel to the US* (Colorado Springs: Eleison, 2008), 51–68.

2. For more information about the Sonrise School, go to www.mustardseedproject.org.

41
PART AND PARCEL

Reflections on John 13:6–11

So He came to Simon Peter. He said to Him, "Lord, do You wash my feet?" . . . "Never shall You wash my feet!" Jesus answered him, "If I do not wash you, you have no part with Me."

—JOHN 13:6, 8

Peter couldn't help his outburst.

Maybe he was first. Maybe he wasn't. No doubt, the longer he waited for Jesus, the more he stewed. There was no way he'd let Him wash his feet. And he told Him so. The moment Jesus knelt in front of him, Peter erupted.

"Lord . . ."

And that was the problem. He knew too much. He knew He was "the Christ, the Son of the Living God" (Matt. 16:16). With his own eyes, he'd seen Jesus transfigured in glory and majesty. With his own ears, he'd heard the voice of God declare from heaven above, "This is My beloved Son, with whom I am well-pleased" (Matt. 17:5).

"You wash my feet?"

Not Him. Not after seeing the winds and waves obey Him. Or seeing Him walk on water, or the way He healed multitudes of people and raised Lazarus after four days in the tomb. No, the Baptist was right. We're not worthy to come to His feet let alone unstrap His sandals and wash them.

Jesus calmed him and said in effect, "You don't understand. But you will. Later."

"Never!" Peter retorted. But it's an odd, confusing response. Wasn't he being humble? Wasn't he telling Jesus he wasn't worthy? His voice kept stressing the "You" and "my." How can "You," the greater, wash "my," the lesser's, feet? The answer, "Never!" He refused Him—bold, brash, and in control. The lesser dictating to the greater.[1]

But what kind of humility is that? Peter was sending mixed signals.

And yet, Jesus was patient with him. In simple terms, He told Peter this washing was everything. It was the only way to be "part" of Jesus and His eternal kingdom. If he wanted to belong, if he wanted "in"—fully in—this was it.

"If I do not wash you, you have no part with Me."

Which meant Peter was faced with a hard reality. How was he to let go of his bold, brash, in-control pride that pushed Jesus away? Had he pulled back his feet so Jesus couldn't touch them? And yet, just the thought of having "no part with Me" caused a spontaneous reaction in him. He suddenly exploded with exuberance. Perhaps he jettisoned his feet out, saying, "Lord, then wash not only my feet, but also my hands and my head."

A big "Yes!" But he still didn't understand what was going on. Not yet.

But for Jesus, it was OK. He took Peter's feet and began. Peter was not like Judas—who was clean on the outside and unclean on the inside. No, Peter was different. Peter was why He came. This night, He would wash his feet with water. The next day, He would wash his soul with His cleansing blood.

And that's why He could say it—and say it strongly, "You are clean!"[2]

As I said, we visited John and Harriet in Rwanda in the spring of 1998.

We flew into the capital city of Kigali, got our luggage, and hoped to see John waiting for us. Instead, he'd sent a clergyman named Ephraim to pick us up. He had a round, gentle face with brightness in his eyes, a gracious smile, and a warm, pastoral disposition that seemed altogether kind.

He greeted us with a handshake and an apology that English wasn't easy for him. He immediately handed us a note from John:

> *You are most welcome in Rwanda. . . . I am very sorry for not being at the airport to meet you. I have an important national meeting to attend. I was asked to give a talk. I will explain on arrival. . . . I have sent Archdeacon Ephraim Semabumba to meet you. The way is well protected. Be at peace.*
>
> *Yours in Christ,*
> *Bishop John Rucyahana*[3]

We got in the car, drove out of Kigali, and took the major roadway to the mountainous northwest. For an hour and a half, we had front-row seats to witness the magnificent beauty of Rwanda's lush terrain, the meticulous architecture of terraced hills and cultivated valleys with rivers cut deep into the landscape and meandering gently on their courses.

This road, this beautiful road, was where John had nearly lost his life in an ambush several months before. I'd just read on the Internet that infiltrators had attacked a minibus only weeks ago—killing everyone. On this very road.

John had written, "The way is well protected. Be at peace." And maybe we would have been if it hadn't been for Ephraim. He was nervous. His eyes kept moving back and forth from the road to the mountainside in an unending, annoying rhythm. He was obviously watching for infiltrators. He was—like us—scared.

The drive couldn't have ended soon enough.

That night, as we sat for dinner with John and Harriet, we learned that John had barely escaped death that afternoon.

He was heading home after work. As he got into his car, some workers asked him for a ride. They didn't want to walk home due to an impending storm. He agreed, drove them to a certain street in town, and dropped them off. Twenty minutes later, after John arrived home, the phone rang.

Rebel forces had just attacked that same street with open gunfire.

"Had we walked home, Bishop," one of the workers said, "we would have most certainly died today."

And for John, it was the same story. He had been there—on that street—only minutes before the shooting. What if the timing had been different? What if he'd stayed there for a while? What if he'd gotten out of his car and lingered in conversation with the workers?

Timing. It was all timing.

He struggled with mixed emotions. Yes, the Lord had been kind to him. But people had just died. Loved ones were now mourning. Fear was now spreading to towns and villages as the news got out. This place was not well protected. It was not safe.

As we went to bed that night, tired from a long plane flight, we could feel the fear. John and Harriet lived in the center of town. With our windows open, we could hear sounds everywhere like a thousand echoes bouncing off the surrounding hills. There was music. Voices. Sometimes shouting.

Then we heard it—*Bang! Bang! Bang! Bang!*

Shots. Real shots. Erilynne and I both sat up, eyes wide open. It sounded close. It could have been down the street. Was it the infiltrators? Had people just been shot?

Were they coming for us?

There was no movement in the house. We wondered if John and Harriet had heard it. Were they awake? We sat there—our hearts racing, scared, waiting for more. But nothing. Some time passed, maybe an hour or two, and it happened again. In the long hours past midnight, our minds tormented us. We kept thinking, at any minute, they'd break into the house—into our room.

We prayed. We waited for the first light of dawn.

"No one ever gets used to it," John told us at breakfast. Who lives like this?

We spent a week there. We traveled to schools, medical clinics, churches, and memorial sites of the genocide. And everywhere we went, we had a military escort. Three men dressed in fatigues, carrying rifles, sent by the local government. They feared we, as Americans, might attract infiltrators. They wanted to protect the residents as well as us. They wanted us safe.

In a world that wasn't safe.

They made us feel like outsiders. We weren't part and parcel of the people's lives, their suffering, or the fear that terrorized their hearts every time the rebels attacked. No, we were visitors. We'd soon be gone. But what if we stayed? What if the Lord called us to step fully "in" and be "part" of their lives?

"How do you do it?" I asked John before we left.

"It may not be easy," he said. "We may not feel comfortable. It may mean we lose people we hold dear. But we do it because we love Jesus. We follow Jesus."

I saw the hurt in his eyes as he said it. I knew he was still grieving Madu and her family. But even then, in his pain, he'd never dream of leaving. He'd go on suffering for as long as his people were suffering. He was part of them, fully part.

But me?

I couldn't help the feeling inside, the ache. I'm not like John. I didn't want the Lord calling us there. I didn't want to live where shots ring out at night and where people live in constant fear. I didn't want "in." I didn't want any "part."

I just wanted to go home.

QUESTIONS FOR REFLECTION

How do we—undeserving and unworthy—receive the Lord's mercy in washing us? What does it mean for you to be "clean" and be a part with Him?

Have you suffered as a Christian? What has it cost you to be "in" and stay "in" as "part" of His people in a rebellious, unsafe world?

NOTES

1. Leon Morris commented that when Peter said "You" it was "emphatic, and in the Greek is followed immediately by 'my,' thus placing the two in sharp contrast." Leon Morris, *The Gospel according to John* (Grand Rapids, MI: Eerdmans, 1971), 617.

2. In verses 8 and 10, we see two aspects of foot-washing. First, it is a saving act. We must receive the Lord's washing to have "part" with Him. Second, it is a sanctifying act. As Christians, we grow in Christ by regular confession, repentance, and need for His daily cleansing in our lives (see 1 John 1:7, 9; 2:1–2).

3. Thaddeus Barnum, *Never Silent: How Third World Missionaries Are Bringing the Gospel to the US* (Colorado Springs: Eleison, 2008), 69–76.

42

IT'S YOUR TURN NOW

~~~

Reflections on John 13:12–17, 34–35

You call Me Teacher and Lord; and you are right,
for so I am. If I then, the Lord and the Teacher, washed
your feet, you also ought to wash one another's feet. . . .
If you know these things, you are blessed if you do them.

—John 13:13–14, 17

When every foot had been washed, and our Lord had finished His work, He did what slaves never do.

He rose, took back His garments, and sat at the table.

Until now, His motion down had been the perfect picture of His story. He'd come down from His eternal glory to become man. Soon enough, He'd go down into the depths of unfathomable down as He endured the fires of Calvary.

But His story wouldn't stay down.

When He'd finished His work on the cross to the full, having taken captive and destroyed the powers of evil, sin, and death, the Father exalted His Son "and bestowed on Him the name which is above every name" (Phil. 2:9).

He rose. That's the full story.

This motion up was the motion of His eternal triumph.

And in rising, He would soon ascend to His Father and take again His garments of glory which He had with Him "before the world was" (John 17:5). But for that moment, in the upper room, the perfect picture was still only a perfect picture. The garments

He took were still His earthly garments. The work, the real work, still had to be done.

But the picture says it all. If we are to rise with Him, we must go down with Him. The way up is never directly up. That's the kingdom of this world. The Devil has infused this fallen creation with the lust for up without telling anyone the real story: His up always comes down. No matter how high, how powerful, how rich and famous, how noble, how memorable, we all come crashing down.

Down into the dust of death and judgment.

But it's different now. If we let Jesus wash us, if we're made clean by Him, then His story becomes our story. If we want up, if we want to be "part" of His eternal triumph, we must bend down. Like Him. Always down.

"If I then, the Lord and the Teacher, washed your feet, you also . . ."

We are to do as He has done for us. Yes, in washing feet. But that, too, is only a picture. He was talking more—much more. He was talking about every aspect of how we treat each other. In the little things. In the big things. In all things.

"A new commandment I give to you, that you love one another, even as I have loved you, that you also love one another" (John 13:34).

He said it at the table that night, but they didn't get it. Not yet. But soon, the Helper, the Holy Spirit, would come and bring to their remembrance all Jesus had said to them. He'd even fill them with His power to do it. But they'd have to have ears to hear.

A simple message. An eternal, unchanging message.

It's your turn now.

A few years later, I met John in a hotel lobby in Pittsburgh on a rainy Sunday afternoon in April. We talked for hours, as old friends do.[1]

By that time, peace had come to Rwanda's northwest, and John was doing everything he could to bring healing and reconciliation to his country. That included his recent election as chairman of Prison Fellowship in Rwanda.

"What's that like for you?" I asked him.

"It isn't easy." The frown between his eyes deepened. He looked at me like he was trying to decide whether he wanted to talk about it or not. "There is sin in my heart."

I looked at him in surprise. I didn't understand.

As John often does, here he painted pictures with his words. He described a field on a hillside overlooking one of the prisons of Rwanda. In the distance, volcanic mountains rise to meet the clouds in the air. Around him are lakes, lush green hills, and workers tilling the land for as far as the eye can see.

The prison below, with soldiers standing at the entrance, marks a sharp contrast to all the beauty around it. He told me there were more than 110,000 prisoners filling the Rwandan jails since the genocide. He has been inside some of them. He has listened to the story of many prisoners.

"They still hear the screaming voices of those they killed," he said. "The scenes replay in their minds. It torments them. It wakes them at night. The guilt is fresh, like an open wound still bleeding. They feel the presence of evil haunting them. The pain presses on them. It's too much for anyone to bear."

I watched as tears filled his eyes.

He told me his first time at the prison was the hardest. He went by invitation. He was asked to preach the gospel in front of a large gathering of prisoners.

"I knew they needed Jesus."

He stopped to wipe his eyes with his handkerchief.

"These murderers are guilty of a great sin. They will never be able to pay for what they did. Only Jesus can save them. They need to know that. They need to know what He did for them at the cross. So I told them plainly, they must run to Jesus, repent of their sin, and beg for His mercy."

I nodded, trying to take it all in.

"And they started to do it," he said. His face twisted in dismay. John then told me that a son of the East African Revival; he knows when the Holy Spirit starts to convict people of sin and move them to saving faith in Jesus Christ. "When I saw that, I reacted. I stopped preaching. They didn't want me to stop. But I couldn't do it."

He told me he ran out of the prison and didn't stop.

"Not until I got to the hillside. Tears were streaming down my face. Pain was gripping my heart. I couldn't believe the depth of anger I felt against them. It shocked and overwhelmed me. But these people are the same kind of people who killed my family. They killed my niece, Madu. They tortured and raped her."

He looked away, his fists clenched.

"What was I doing preaching to her killers? I tell you the pain was too great for me. I fell on my knees and wept. I thought I wanted those men to know Jesus, but it's not true. Why would He want to save those men? How could He forgive them for what they did to me, my family, and my country?"

He looked at me like I was supposed to answer.

"Can you see the sin in my heart?" he asked. "If anybody needed to run to Jesus and repent, it was me. The desire for revenge was choking me. I was no different than those prisoners. I was locked behind the bars of my own unforgiveness. So I prayed, 'Lord Jesus Christ, help me. I must forgive the killers of my family, and I can't do it. The pain is too great. The hurt is too deep.'"

He grabbed my hand. He was still grieving.

"I couldn't stop the crying," he said. "But in my tears, the Lord reminded me of what He did on the cross. Did He turn away from His killers? No, He faced them. He looked them straight in the eyes and cried out from the midst of His pain, 'Father, forgive them; for they do not know what they are doing.' How could He do that? How could He forgive them while He was in pain?" he asked me.

I shook my head. I didn't know.

He let go of my hand. His face was still wet from tears as he said, "When Jesus Christ was hanging on the tree, stripped, beaten, mocked, despised, nails tearing through His flesh, nails in His feet, and a crown of thorns on His head, from within that pain He cried, 'Forgive! Forgive!'

"And I knew the Lord was telling me, 'Now it's your turn.' If He didn't wait until the pain was gone, we can't wait.

We must do as He did and forgive while we're in pain. This is what Christians do, and He gives us the power to do it."

He leaned back in his chair. He told me he how he got up, went back down that hillside, back into the prison, back into the room filled with prisoners, and loved them with the love of Jesus.

"To this day, I go to the prison in tears. It isn't easy for me."

He reached for my hand again and looked at me. He was wondering if I understood, and if I did, did I realize the same is true for me too—it's true for all Christians.

It's our turn now.

QUESTIONS FOR REFLECTION

Jesus commanded us to love one another. Do we know how to bend down? Do we love this way? How would we impact our communities if we did?

Is it possible, in human strength, to love and forgive while we're still in pain? But, in His power and strength, can we do it? Isn't it our turn now?

NOTE

1. Thaddeus Barnum, *Never Silent: How Third World Mission-aries Are Bringing the Gospel to the US* (Colorado Springs: Eleison, 2008), 257, 273–276.

43

OUR COLD HEARTS

~~~

Reflections on Luke 22:24–30

*And there arose also a dispute among them as to
which one of them was regarded to be greatest.*

—LUKE 22:24

It makes no sense whatsoever.

*Sometime after supper—Were they still in the upper room?
Had Judas already left? Was Jesus in earshot?—it started again.
They argued over which of them was the greatest, who did Jesus
favor more, who'd sit at His side in His kingdom?*

It always dogged them.

*Soon after the transfiguration, as they neared Capernaum,
they got caught. It was the same conversation. Like always, they
made sure Jesus couldn't hear. But this time, somehow, He knew
what they were talking about and confronted them.*

*"You want to be first? Be last. Be servant of all" (see Mark
9:33–37).*

*Eventually, James and John got up the courage to ask Him
directly, "Grant us to sit, one at Your right hand and one at Your
left, in Your glory." It angered the others. It provoked Jesus to
repeat the story: "The greatest serve." And to add, "I am not here
to be served but to serve and to give My life as a ransom for
many" (see Mark 10:35–45).*

They didn't get it.

Even now, just after He washed their feet, they didn't get it.

In a few hours, the powers of darkness would descend on Him. The crown of thorns would be pressed on His head, and the nails of Calvary would pierce into His hands and feet. From heaven, the Father would lay on Him "the iniquity of us all" (Isa. 53:6). And down He'd go into suffering and death—the perfect Lamb, the perfect offering to "take away the sin of the world" (John 1:29). Down and down and down.

If only they understood.

But they didn't. They were arguing again—on this night of all nights. It was still all they could talk about. Up and up and up—which of them was greatest? Who would be recognized more than others? Who would have power and fame and glory?

Their hearts were cold.

But not for long. Jesus had promised Peter, when He washed his feet, "You don't get it now. But you will later." He'd have to do His work first. He'd have to suffer the torment of Calvary and, then, on the third day, rise again, go to His disciples, and breathe His resurrected life into their bodies. That's what they needed—new, born-again life. Their souls filled by the Holy Spirit. Only then would they understand the secret of the kingdom of God.

He has called us to serve. Always serve. Just as He served.

And that's exactly what happened. On Easter night, our Lord breathed on His disciples and said, "Receive the Holy Spirit" (John 20:22). And with it came the charge: "As the Father has sent Me, I also send you" (John 20:21).

These Christians! They were different. They had a new heart. Not like the old one. They raced to serve. They longed for the lowest place—which is the highest place. All because He who is the highest took the lowest and made the lowest the highest. That's why they served. Always served. Just as He served.

Their hearts—cold no more.

As the years passed, John and I grew more distant. Not because anything happened between us. Life got busy, that's all.

Bishop John became more prominent in Rwanda, serving on committees locally and nationally and traveling to all parts of the world to help his country recover. And, for me, I had more responsibility than I could handle.

We'd correspond. We'd call each other on the phone. When we'd finally meet, it was usually to attend a meeting.

A movement had begun in our denomination that resulted in strengthening the bonds between the African and American church. We, on our part, needed the strength of their preaching and faith that was tested by war, poverty, and persecution. They, on their part, wanted us to build relationships with their pastors, churches, schools, orphans, widows, and seminaries.

Neither of us led the movement. But we were an integral part of it, coming alongside great church leaders who gave themselves to this work. For over a decade, we saw the Lord's favor. What John and I had together—an African and an American bound together in Jesus Christ—was now being shared by many. It thrilled us beyond words. But then, something happened.

The coldness came.

Some of the principal leaders in the movement began to disagree with each other over matters of vision and strategy. Soon enough, it intensified. It became personal. People got hurt. Longtime relationships in Christ—among well-loved Christian leaders—strained and broke. Division and heartache soon plagued a movement born for the glory of God.

John and some of his colleagues did their best to bring the message of biblical forgiveness and reconciliation— the same message that was bringing life to a post-genocide Rwanda. At the same time, many of us in the US did our part to beg for the same thing. We tried to mediate. We tried to stop it.

But it didn't work. Division came.

As always, division is shrouded in complexities. There are sides to each story. Both need to be heard. It's how we assess who is right and who is wrong, so we can decide which side we'll take. But, in truth, it's not complicated at all.

We chose not to love each other.

Deep in my soul, I prize this foot-washing story. If we are Christians, if the resurrected life of Jesus Christ fills our mortal bodies, He commands us to do as He did to us. We strip our garments, we robe as servants, we grab a basin and towel, get down on our knees, and wash and wash and wash. Until we love again.

We're not allowed to divide. Not in Christ. Not as Christians.

But we did. And soon enough, the coldness came to me. I too was on "one side" of the argument. And though I tried to speak well of those on "the other side," it hurt too much. People I love were hurt. People I love did the hurting. And though in principle I tried to do what was right, I couldn't stop it.

The rush of coldness filled my heart too.

It was, in many ways, imperceptible. I was very busy as a clergyman. I could do my job, and do it well, all the while pretending this story never happened. I could easily make believe I had no part in the division whatsoever and pretend I was fully, completely unaffected by it all. Coldness is like that. But I couldn't sustain it.

I had too many friends like Bishop John. He'd call, we'd talk for an hour, and at the end of the call, he'd always remind me not to let unforgiveness grab my heart and shape my life in Christ. "It's a choice, you know?" he'd warn.

"I know," I'd say, and promise I'd choose it every day. But, in truth, I didn't know what that meant. Not really.

Not until my wife was diagnosed with a peculiar rheumatoid, autoimmune condition that resulted in open, non-healing wounds on her lower right leg near the ankle. With no known treatment or cure.

And so, we began. Every evening before dinner.

We have a basket. It is filled with everything needed to change her dressing. One of us, depending on the night, gets it ready. And then, it's my turn. I get to go down on my knees, go to her feet, and begin the process.

I start by cutting off the old bandage. I then wash her foot and the wounds with saline—drying it all with gauze. I apply the medicine the doctor gave us to care for the skin and prevent infection. And then I cover the wounds with a lubricated pad, followed by gauze, and then a bandage wrapping around her foot and held on by paper tape.

We do this every night.

Not for a month. Or a year. But, at this writing, it's been over seven years.

It has taught me the secret of God's kingdom. And it's real, physical, practical. As real as a basin of water, a towel girded around the waist, and the choice—always the choice—to go down to the feet of our brothers and sisters in Christ and wash them every day. No matter what "side" they have taken.

We love as the Lord Jesus loved us.

No matter how complex our disagreements. And for us, in this movement, it has worked. Nearly all have reconciled. And for those who haven't, we continue to do what we can, when we can, to turn swords that once pierced hearts into towels.

We're learning to wash, beginning with our family in Christ. Then to the people in our communities. Towels are everything. They define mission. And as we do, Easter morning fills us again and surprise!

Our hearts are cold no more.

QUESTIONS FOR REFLECTION

Why were the disciples plagued by the question of who was the greatest? Why on this night? Is it still a lead issue today? In you? In the church?

Why do we experience this coldness as Christians today? What can we proactively do to turn swords into towels and wash until hearts return to Jesus?

PART 7

FIVE
FRIENDS

44

MERCY AT THE MAT

Reflections on Mark 2:1–3

And they came, bringing to Him a paralytic,
carried by four men.

—Mark 2:3

Everything inside me wants to interview these four men. Who were they? Were they brothers? Were they old school chums? Were they four very different men, different ages, who all spent time with those tossed away by society? Was that how they met? While caring for others? All because they shared a passion for God and His one demand on our soul.

And how did they meet this man on the mat in particular?

Who was he? How did he become paralyzed? Did anybody else care for him? What is it about him that drew these four men together? Was it simply because they loved him? They'd spent time with him, visiting when they could, taking turns to help him when no one else did. Is that it? Big hearts of mercy and love.

Maybe it is that simple. They were what he needed most—friends.

Real friends. So when a day like this came, he was their first thought.

Jesus was back. All of Capernaum was buzzing. If they cared only for themselves, they could run to the house where Jesus was speaking. They could get front row seats. Just weeks before, Jesus had been there, healing the sick and casting out demons (Mark 1:21–34). And then He was gone, traveling from town to town. Would He do the same now?

And the men did run—the second they heard Jesus was back in town. But not to the house. Not to get a seat for themselves. But for their friend.

They needed to get him to Jesus.

Why? Isn't it obvious? These four men loved the man on the mat. Mercy and care, kindness and compassion, had been there long before they knew of Jesus. They wouldn't have been ready otherwise. How else could they have known what to do and where to go when a day like this came? But they did.

They went to get their friend.

They saw something. They knew something. Mercy is more than sacrificially caring for the immediate needs of those in need. Mercy is more than restoring the dignity and honor of every human being. Yes, it is those things. It is always those things. But mercy leaps beyond here and now and brings about the one thing in life that's most important.

Mercy brings us to God.

I first met Walt and Carol Pittman after church on a Sunday morning. They were in their early fifties with two children in high school and one in college. They loved our church and told me they wanted to make it their home.

A few weeks later, Walt came to our men's Bible study.

We met every Friday morning from 6:15 to 7:30. As the months passed, Walt slowly shared parts of his life with us. The most astonishing, most impressive thing about him was his passion for senior citizens. "They were there for us," he'd explain. "Now it's time for us to be there for them."

Nearly every Friday, Walt had us pray for someone he'd met that week.

"Pray for Josephine," he told us one day. As he shared her story, it sounded strangely familiar to all the other stories he told us. She was alone, forgotten by her family, and without an advocate to speak for her in the nursing home. Somehow, Walt had gotten her daughter's phone number and left messages. "She lives ten miles away," he lamented, "and never visits her own mother."

We had four nursing homes in town. Walt visited each one.

"Is it your job?" we asked him.

Turns out, he was an administrator at one of the city hospitals. But, early on, he was trained as a social worker. He saw firsthand the neglect and abuse of seniors by families, health care professionals, and government agencies.

"Sometimes all that's needed is someone who cares," he taught us.

Within a few months, at Walt's leading, our church hosted our first seniors' luncheon. He gave us a list of some thirty names that included people in nursing homes as well as local shut-ins. He got our men's group to coordinate the event and rally the church behind it. It was a delightful time and the first of many to come.

Walt had lit a passion in our church to care for seniors.

At some point, he and I had lunch together.

As we shared our stories, I couldn't help but sense a certain sadness about him. A hurt of some kind. He was a gentle, kind man, reserved, unassuming, and easy to talk to. He wanted to know as much about me as I did about him.

"Tell me two things," I said at one point during the lunch. "How did you come to faith in Christ, and when did He give you a love for the elderly?"

The story of his conversion was simply spectacular. He had no Christian upbringing whatsoever. If anything, his family was antagonistic toward God and organized religion. In his early twenties, a friend invited him to hear evangelist Billy Graham at Three Rivers Stadium in downtown Pittsburgh.

"That's all it took," he said with a smile. "Jesus saved me that day. The man I was and the man I became were two very different people, believe you me! Then, shortly after, my friend took me to his church. That's where I met Carol."

"So what were you like before?" I inquired.

"Bitter and angry," he said. "Resentful, I suppose. I had a tough childhood."

He slowly unpacked the story of his father. "He worked twelve hours or more a day, six days a week. On Sundays, he golfed. We basically never saw him. And when we did, he was mean to us. Mean to my sister and me. Mean to our mom. I have no good memories of him growing up. All I remember is him yelling at me and hitting me. Never, not once, did he tell me he loved me or was proud of me. Even my mom. I have no memory of him being nice to her."

"Is he still alive?"

Walt nodded, and I could see the sadness in his eyes.

"Which partly answers your other question," he said. "For a few years, my grandfather—on my dad's side— came to live with us. He had the beginning stages of dementia. Eventually, he went into a nursing home. My dad went to see him—I'm talking about his own father!— maybe once or twice in eight years. My mom went nearly every day, and often we'd go with her after school."

He shook his head, still reeling in disgust.

"How's your mom now?"

As he talked about her, all I could picture was this dark, foreboding character of her husband hovering over her. Always there—always tormenting.

"My mom and sister eventually came to faith in Christ," he shared. "My sister and I still do our best to get her more involved at church or in family events. But she rarely does. She can go out. She can do anything she wants. But it's like my dad has this hold on her somehow. Even now, after all these years."

"So, do you ever see your dad?"

"All the time. I made the decision years ago I was going to love him whether he wanted it or not, whether he loved me back or not. Of course, nothing has changed. He doesn't care whether I'm alive or dead. But I figure, I don't have to make the same choices he made."

He looked at me with despairing but courageous eyes.

And for a split second, I saw Walt as one of the four men in the gospel story. There at the side of the crippled man, showing kindness and relentless mercy.

Even to the man who cripples his own soul.

QUESTIONS FOR REFLECTION

Why do you think these four men cared more for the man on the mat than getting to Jesus themselves? Do you have the same heart for those in need?

Walt's love for seniors came out of his experience with his father and grandfather. What is your experience? To whom can you show relentless mercy and love?

45

MERCY AT THE HOUSE

Reflections on Mark 2:1–4

And they came, bringing to Him a paralytic, carried by four men.
Being unable to get to Him because of the crowd.

—MARK 2:3–4

The man on the mat—we can't see his face.

We know nothing about him, not really. We don't know his name, his age, his background. No idea the nature of his overall medical condition. Of all the crippled in Capernaum, was he the most critical? Was his life in danger?

There's a reason we don't know. This story isn't first about him.

It's about the four men at each corner of his mat. We can almost see their faces. There was expectation in them—anticipation! You see, we know something about them. They had the gift of faith. Faith to believe their prayers for their friend were going to be answered. They knew it. They believed it (see Mark 2:5).

No doubt we can almost see it in their feet.

It wasn't a casual stroll, was it? It wasn't like they were walking in a funeral procession or dragging their feet to someplace they didn't want to go. Wasn't there a briskness about them, maybe even a slow run? Like men who couldn't wait to get there?

Were they talking? Were they praying? Were they already singing praise to God for what He was about to do for their friend?

Faith is like that, you know. It sees before it happens. It leaps with joy as if what's promised in the future is already here.

This story is about them—their faith, their confidence.

Already at the house, Jesus was preaching. People were listening. Perhaps there was already a palpable sense in the house that He was filled to the brim with the power to heal (see Luke 5:17–26, especially v. 17). If ever mercy had a source, it's here—in this Person. On His face. In His words. In His heart for the people.

Could those by the door feel it? What about those outside? The five men were almost there.

Down one street, down another. Was it Simon and Andrew's house again? And then, suddenly, it happened. They saw it. They saw the mass of people surrounding the house. What was that moment like for them? Did their hearts sink? Could they feel disappointment flood their souls?

Just like before, "the whole city had gathered at the door" (Mark 1:33).

They'd never get to Him—never. There was no room inside, no room outside, and too many people in front of them wanting to see Jesus just as much as they did.

So, I wonder, did they think through their options? Should they try to muscle their way through the crowd? Should they look for someone who could help them? Maybe a politician or a policeman who would grant them favor and push them to the front? They needed to get inside, but it was utterly impossible. Not that day. Too many roadblocks.

There's nothing worse than this—when our faith faces something bigger than us. We get that pit in our stomachs. That ache in our souls. What we expected from God—what we most believed He'd do—is suddenly stolen from us. And we stand there, confused, crushed, not knowing what to do next.

So close to Jesus. So far away.

"For years, Dad and I didn't talk," Walt told me. We were still at lunch. "But when Christ came into my life and I met Carol, things changed."

He smiled at the mention of Carol.

"She wouldn't marry me, you know. Not until I dealt with my father. She said my anger against him was controlling me. And she was right."

"Smart woman," I commented.

"We talked a lot about it," he went on. "I told her I wanted him out of my life. I figured it was better for me that way—have nothing to do with him. She said she didn't think my plan was working. I was just as angry, just as resentful. She'd say, 'You push him away but he's still there, stronger than ever.'

"It took a while, but eventually we realized the Lord had another plan in mind. If we wanted to be witnesses of Christ in his life, we needed to pursue him, get involved—care for him, love him, do whatever we could when we could."

"That must have been hard for you," I remarked.

"It was, but it changed me. I didn't do it perfectly, mind you. There were times, especially early on, when he'd provoke me, I'd react, and we'd fight it out like old times, maybe worse. I had to learn I couldn't do this without the Lord.

"But here's the good news," he said, almost playfully, with a grin.

"Carol married you!" I shot back quickly.

"Yeah! Well, besides that. Our being there for Dad made a huge impact on both my mom and sister. Years later, we got to talk to them about faith in Jesus."

"But not your dad?" I asked.

"Dad's a different story," he said painfully.

The sadness was still there, etched in his face.

"More than anything, I wanted my father to know Christ. Carol and I prayed all the time. We even went to our pastor and asked him what we should do. He told us two things. First, never stop praying. And second, be sensitive to the Holy Spirit. He said, 'Watch for Him. Wait till He gives you an opportunity.'

"So, we did. But it was frustrating. My dad's a hard man. I'd try to break him out of his routine—visit him at work, take him to lunch, play golf with him. I told him I wanted time with him, just to get to know him better."

Walt sat there, shaking his head.

"He had no interest whatsoever. He told me to buzz off. If I needed a friend, or some long-lost father figure, 'bleeding hearts are a dime a dozen,' he'd say and tell me to go find one. But not him. He wanted nothing to do with me."

"Ouch," I said quietly. "I'm sorry."

"Yeah, thanks. If it weren't for Carol, I'd have given up a long time ago. But she kept us going. We never stopped praying for him. Never stopped doing whatever we could for him. And I bet we did that for ten years. Maybe eleven. Anyway, it took that long for me to finally present the gospel to him."

"So the opportunity came?"

"Yeah, and in a hospital of all places."

He paused a bit, as if the memory was hard for him.

"When our third child, Zane, was about five, his appendix burst. He was in ICU for maybe a week or so. He had all kinds of complications that made it worse for him. At one point, we thought we might lose him.

"A day or two after his first surgery, out of the blue, my dad shows up at the hospital. We couldn't believe it. I can still remember the look on my mother's face. So he goes over to Zane and just stands there at his bedside. Maybe five minutes or more. Before he leaves, he says to me, 'You OK, Son?'

"I say, 'Not really, Dad.'

"He nods back as if he understands. He did the same with Carol and my mom, like he was genuinely sympathetic. We'd never seen him like that before.

"Two days later, when Zane was at his worst, he shows up again. This time, he stands next to Zane and holds his hand. I'm standing on the other side of the bed, and I swear I see tears in his eyes. About an hour later, I'm walking out of the ICU and pass the waiting room. I look in and see him sitting there, staring out the window.

"Dad?"

"He asks if Zane's any better. I tell him he's not—not yet, anyway. And for the next half hour, my dad opens his heart to me. It's like this little window popped up for the first time in our lives. He tells me he's afraid Zane's going to die and what then? He says he could never handle something like that.

"Then he asks me, point blank, 'How do you do it, Son? How do you cope?'

"And I knew—this was it. I got to tell my dad about Jesus Christ. It came with such ease. I can't tell you how strongly I felt the Lord with me. I told him how Jesus saved me the night I heard Billy Graham speak and how He's changed my life ever since. I told Dad I loved him and I wanted him to know Jesus too."

Walt looked at me, almost wincing with pain.

"But he wanted nothing to do with it. He shut down so fast. His face turned hard. All he could say was, 'That's not for me, Son.' And the man I saw in the waiting room that day, I haven't seen since—which breaks my heart.

"I just want to bring him to Jesus."

QUESTIONS FOR REFLECTION

In Mark 2:5, we know these four men have faith. And yet, they faced impossible roadblocks to get to Jesus. When have you felt crushed in your faith? When have you experienced these roadblocks?

Consider the pastor's counsel: Caring for souls requires prayer, sensitivity to the Holy Spirit, and readiness. Can you apply this to people in your life who need His mercy but are hardened to Him?

46

FIERCE DETERMINATION

Reflections on Mark 2:4–5

Being unable to get to Him because of the crowd,
they removed the roof above Him; and when they
had dug an opening, they let down the pallet on which
the paralytic was lying. And Jesus seeing their faith . . .

—MARK 2:4–5

There were options.

They could have taken him home, waited for another day, and tried again. Or they could stay there—at the back of the crowd—and wait it out. Maybe something would happen, something unexpected that would allow them time with Jesus.

Or they could push their way through the crowd.

It's what happens in a time of crisis. Something fierce comes into our souls, this sense of urgency and desperation. This need to survive. We have little care for other people. We push. We force our way past them until we get what we need.

Is that how these four men felt about their friend?

Was it already happening? Could they see it? Were people trying to push their way through the crowd? The news on the street was that Jesus of Nazareth had become so popular, everybody was pressing in on Him—just to touch Him (see Mark 3:10; 5:31).

Should they?

But then it happened. Sometimes when faced with the impossible, God opens our eyes to see the possible. He gives wisdom. He gives faith—not simply faith in Him. Nor faith that He has power to heal. But faith that knows exactly what to do next.

They knew what to do—the roof!

Were there stairs on the side of the house?[1] How did they get their friend up there? How did they break through the roof? How did they know where Jesus was sitting? Was the crowd angry with them for jumping the line or, instead marveling at the spectacle of it all?

No matter. They had eyes of faith. They saw the impossible possible and with a fierce determination, they got on the roof and started tearing it apart.

I wonder, did it take five minutes or thirty? When did the people inside realize what was happening? When did Jesus stop teaching? Did some of the roof come down on top of them—on top of Him?

And what was it like when the digging was done?

Did joy fill their hearts as they grabbed the mat and slowly, carefully, lowered their friend down into the safe hands of those closest to Jesus? And what was it like to see Jesus? Or to see Jesus see their friend for the first time? Or to see Jesus look up and see them?

He saw their faces—the four friends. And in seeing, He saw faith! Faith that breaks through roofs. Faith that believes He can heal their friend. And it found favor in His eyes as He turned toward the paralytic.

What a moment! Especially for the four men. They got to see it all.

A few years passed.

Walt often talked about his dad at the Friday morning men's Bible study and would ask us to pray for him. Nothing

had changed. "If anything, it's worse," he'd say. "He's in his midseventies, working as hard as ever, married to Mom for fifty-six years, and barely talks to her—or any of us."

For the most part, Walt rarely showed his worry about his dad. But at times it was there on his face, in his heart, like a man with a pronounced limp in his soul.

Then one night, about a quarter past nine, he called me at home.

"We're in the ER," he told me. "Dad's had a heart attack. It's bad. Would you mind coming down?"

It took me a little over twenty minutes to get there. Walt and Carol, his mom, his sister and her husband, and a few of the older grandchildren were in the waiting room. The doctor hadn't come to see them yet.

"They're still working on him," Walt told me.

He asked if we could pray together, which we did. Each grabbing the other's hand. Walt's prayer was the most desperate: "Lord, please don't let him die. Not yet. Not until he knows You. Please, Jesus, Lord, have mercy on our dad."

A little while later, the doctor came out.

He told us they were able to resuscitate him. "I'm not sure for how long," he added. "His heart is severely damaged." He explained as much as he could, answered questions, and let two people at a time go in to see him.

Over the next few days, the news grew worse. "If we try to surgically repair the heart," the doctor informed them, "we'll lose him. He's not strong enough." He promised to monitor any progress and to keep Walt's dad comfortable.

"What concerns me more," Walt told me, "is his real heart." We were standing outside his dad's ICU room.

"He's pushing us away. He's able to speak. He talks to the nurses and doctors when they come in. He's all there—sound mind. Knows what's going on. Knows he's dying. But with us? He says almost nothing.

"So this morning, my sister, mom, and I stood around his bed. We told him how much we love him. Mom said things I've never heard her say. She talked about when they first met, things they did when they were young, things he used to say to her. He listened but could barely look at her."

"He had no response?" I asked.

"Not really. I mean, it's not like he was rude. He was Dad—distant, cold, uncaring. I don't know how Mom does it."

He shook his head as tears welled up in his eyes.

"I've got to talk to him again. I have to at least try. I can't let him die like this. But he's not going to listen, is he? Not the way he is now. I keep thinking about the story of Andy and his grandfather. Do you remember?"

I did. All too well.

Andy was a college student. Maybe early twenties. A few summers back, he came to our men's Bible study and asked us to pray for his grandfather, who was dying. He was almost at the point of sobbing for his "Pops" to know Jesus. "He hates God. I mean, hates Him."

Andy had asked me to go with him to the nursing home and talk to him. And we went, several times before he died. Once, twice, three times I pressed in and told him the good news of the gospel and what happens to us when we die.

He wanted nothing to do with it. He cursed God, even to his dying breath.

"I don't want that for my dad," Walt said impatiently.

I nodded. I understood.

"But I don't know what to do," he cried, the tears coming more freely. "I'll be real honest here. I'm afraid if I try, that'll be it. He'll do what he always does—rip me apart and turn away. Is that how I want it to end between us?"

I put my hand on his shoulder and began to pray.

We asked the Lord to breathe faith into his soul. Faith that knows exactly what to do next—and when to do it—and how to do it. Faith that was strong, fierce, filled with mercy, and sent from heaven above.

He called the next morning.

"I'm ready," he said, his voice relaxed and calm. "I don't know how Dad will respond. But what I'm asking for is very simple. Years ago, when Zane was sick, I saw my dad—my real dad—in the hospital waiting room. I know he's there, somewhere beneath that calloused, hard shell of his. All I need are the right tools to dig through it and find him again. That's how I want you to pray."

He asked me to call the men in the Bible study and get them to pray too.

"If I can have that—that's all, just that—then I can present the gospel to him one more time. What happens after that is between him and Jesus."

It was there—and beautiful. A God-given faith where nothing is impossible.

QUESTIONS FOR REFLECTION

When has the Lord given you faith in the moment? Faith to know what to do next? Are there "roof" stories in your life when the impossible becomes possible and you're filled with fierce determination?

Have you ever prayed for wisdom, for faith, in how to present your loved one to Jesus? For Walt and Andy, it required trusting Him with what happens next. Can you do that? Have you done that?

NOTE

1. Commentary author William L. Lane suggests, "They ascended a stairway on the side of the house to the flat roof which they broke open." William Lane, *The Gospel of Mark*, The New International Commentary of the New Testament (Grand Rapids, MI: Eerdmans, 1974), 93.

47

FIVE FRIENDS PLUS ONE

Reflections on Mark 2:5–10 and Luke 5:17–24

*Seeing their faith, He said, "Friend, your sins are
forgiven you." The scribes and Pharisees began to reason,
saying, "Who is this man who speaks blasphemies?
Who can forgive sins, but God alone?"*

—LUKE 5:20–21

*Did you know there were other paralytics in the house that
day? Paralytics not of body—but of soul. They, too, experienced
the "power of the Lord" (Luke 5:17) that rested on Jesus.*

*They heard Him preach with more wisdom than King
Solomon; with more authority than Moses; more power than
Elijah; more righteousness than Noah, Daniel, and Job; and
with more unction than the greatest prophets the world has
ever known from Enoch to John the Baptist and Abel to
Zechariah.*

*But it seems to have made no impact on them whatsoever.
It's exactly, Jesus said, what Isaiah foretold: "You will keep on
hearing, but will not understand; you will keep on seeing, but
will not perceive; for the heart of this people has become dull"
(Matt. 13:14–15; see also Isa. 6:9–10).*

There are no guarantees.

*These men, scribes and Pharisees, are not described in the
gospel accounts as friends of Jesus. Rather, they're the ones
who, soon enough, would set their sights on trying to destroy*

Him (see Mark 3:4–6). Of all people, they'd reject any notion that they too were paralytics—just like the man on the mat.

It was time.

Jesus, having seen the faith of the men on the roof for their friend, delightfully calls the man on the mat His friend too: "Friend, your sins are forgiven you."

But it's strange, isn't it? Why doesn't He heal the man of his physical ailment? Why declare that his sins have been forgiven? What's He doing? Is it possible He's diagnosing the real cause of the paralysis? Is it possible His words, if heard, really heard by all the paralytics in the house that day, would have healed them too—all of them?

But no, these other paralytics were hardened and they proved it. At once, in the quiet of their hearts, they opposed Him. They didn't say it, but they were convinced He had just blasphemed. And Jesus knew it. He knew exactly what they were thinking and confronted them with it by asking, "Why are you reasoning [these things] in your hearts?" (Luke 5:22).

They didn't answer. He pressed in deeper, making it worse for them.

"The Son of Man has authority on earth to forgive sins" (Luke 5:24).

If only they could receive it. The cure for their souls was standing right in front of them. But no, they refused. Not so the man on the mat. He did receive. Though still paralyzed in body, his soul was now forgiven and free. The power of sin over him now broken.

A gift from Jesus, the Son of Man, who just called him His friend.

In the early evening, Walt sent a text to my phone. It said simply, **Just sent you an e-mail.** I opened it and found he'd written me a letter:

Thad,

I got to the hospital after ten. I'd asked Mom and my sister Ellie to come at noon. I told them I wanted time with Dad alone. They were fine with it.

First thing out of his mouth, "Where are Ellie and your mom?"

I told him, "They're coming later, Dad. Just you and me for a while."

He figured it out. "So this is it, huh? Say what you've got to say before your old man drops dead? Is that it? Well, get it over with, Son. Do what you gotta do." Almost mad, he turned his head to the window and tried to shut me out.

I pushed his leg over and sat on the bed next to him.

"Remember when Zane was sick, Dad? Remember when you came to the hospital to see him? I saw something in you I'd never seen before. You loved Zane. I mean, really loved him. You thought he was going to die and you were upset. We talked about it, remember, in the waiting room? Well, in the same way, that's how I feel about you, Dad. I don't want you to die."

He was staring blankly now.

"I guess if I were really honest, I'd tell you I was a little jealous. I don't think you ever loved me like that. Or Ellie. Or Mom. At least, I never saw it.

"I was so mad at you growing up. I couldn't wait till I graduated high school to get out of the house. I swore I'd never come back. You said you'd pay for college but I didn't want it, remember that? I did it myself. Every penny. Working nights and weekends. Anything, just to be done with you.

"But not Mom. I'd visit when you weren't around. And she saw it. She saw the anger and hatred in me. It was eating me alive, and I didn't care because it wasn't my fault—that's what I told myself. It was you. I always blamed you."

He had no reaction at all.

"But all that changed for me. I told you that in the waiting room."

I doubted he was even listening.

"A friend of mine invited me to hear this preacher. To this day, I don't know how it happened, but sitting there listening to him, I realized I was wrong. I'd been blaming you all this time when I should've blamed myself. I needed to own the fact that I was mean and hateful because of me. My choice. Not yours.

"That night, the preacher told us to own our own sin and tell God we were sorry. Sorry for our sins—for my sins. He told us how to pray and ask Jesus Christ to come into our lives. And I did. I asked Him to forgive me and change my heart."

By this time, his eyes closed. Like he was completely done with me.

"I still wanted nothing to do with you. Soon after, I went to church and met Carol. She's the one who forced the issue. Did you know, Dad, she wouldn't marry me until I got myself right with you? She said, 'Not until you love him from the heart—really love him—whether he ever loves you back or not.'"

If you can believe this, he actually opened his eyes and looked at me.

"And that's been my choice ever since. So when I say, 'I love you, Dad,' I mean it. When I say, 'I don't want you to die,' I mean it. And more than anything, I don't care what you think of me. I care about Ellie and Mom. Do you feel anything for them, Dad? Like you do for Zane? If you do, they need to know soon."

Right then, I saw him—that man I saw in the waiting room years ago.

"And so does God."

The moment I said "God," he turned his eyes away.

"You've never given Him the time of day. Here you are, about to meet your Maker, and you turn away even at the mention of His name. But, Dad, I'm going to be really selfish here. When I die and go to heaven, I want you there. Do you hear me? That means you have to act like a man and own the wrong in your heart. Why is that hard to do? I need you to get right with Him, Dad."

He looked back at me. Like he heard me.

I lost it. I didn't mean to, but I did. I reached for a tissue on his side table and tried to hold it in, but I *couldn't. Next thing I knew, I felt his hand coming around my neck and bringing me close—against his chest. He held me there. He let me cry until I couldn't cry anymore. I pulled away and told him I'm sorry. I looked at him. I couldn't believe it.*

He had tears in his eyes.

"Tell me what I need to do, Son," he said.

So, I did. I told him exactly how I prayed all those years ago. He nodded and asked me to help him pray too.

Almost naturally, he grabbed my hand and held it. I looked at him, and I saw far more than I ever saw in that waiting room. For the first time, we are what we were meant to be—father and son. And more.

We are friends.

Walt

QUESTIONS FOR REFLECTION

What does it mean to be paralyzed in soul? Does the Isaiah 6:9–10 passage apply to us? If so, how can we receive this gift of mercy that forgives our sin?

How did the Lord's mercy work first in Walt's heart? How did it change his attitude toward his dad? How did it make this conversation even possible? Is this same mercy at work in you?

48

HIS TENDER MERCY

Reflections on Mark 2:9–10

"Which is easier, to say to the paralytic, 'Your sins are forgiven';
or to say, 'Get up, and pick up your pallet and walk'?
But so that you may know that the Son of Man has authority
on earth to forgive sins—" He said to the paralytic,
"I say to you, get up, pick up your pallet and go home."

—MARK 2:9–11

Was Jesus' question too hard for them?

There they sat, refusing to answer. Odd; they should know. There have always been magicians, enchanters, and sorcerers who, engaging the dark powers of Satan, have been able to perform great signs and wonders.

But no one can rescue the soul for God but God.

Why not say it? "It's easier to heal the body than the soul." But they didn't, even though, one could argue, they just saw it happen with their own eyes. Jesus, with a word, lifted the weight of sin from the paralytic's soul and pronounced him forgiven.

But seeing, they didn't see.

So Jesus did, for the first time, what He hadn't done before. He announced himself. He told them His title as "Son of Man"— one that comes from the pages of Scripture. They'd understand immediately He was declaring himself to be the One foretold by Daniel: "I saw in the night visions, and behold, with the clouds of heaven there came one like a son of man. . . . And to him was given dominion, and glory and a kingdom, that all the peoples, nations, and languages should serve him; his dominion is an ever-lasting dominion which shall not pass away, and his kingdom is one that shall not be destroyed" (Dan. 7:13–14 ESV).

If they could understand this, they'd know why He had authority on earth to forgive sins. But they stared at Him—unresponsive. Why wouldn't they engage Him?

But they didn't. So Jesus turned to His new friend on the mat. He'd already given him the greatest gift of all—mercy to his soul. Mercy that would last for all eternity. Now it was time to do the easier work—mercy that cares for his physical needs.

But still, it's a more visible gift. Would that make a difference? If these men saw the physical power of God heal the man on the mat, would they believe? Would their hearts soften? Is this how they'd come to know for certain the Son of Man could heal them too?

Jesus made His move. He wasn't like the magicians and sorcerers with their rituals and incantations. He was altogether different, whether anyone understood it or not. He was the Son of Man. He had been granted all authority by His Father. All He had to do was speak. That was all. Nothing more.

Just the sound—and the tender mercy of God came again.

The following week, Walt communicated mostly by e-mail. "I'm keeping a diary and will send you installments," he wrote. And that's what he did.

Tuesday night—August 13, the day after his talk with his dad:

I woke up discouraged this morning. A little while after we prayed together, Dad was taken down to radiology.

He was there a couple of hours. Not sure why it took so long. Then they decided to transfer him from ICU to a private room. All of it was too much for him. Last night, he needed sleep, not visitors.

I started thinking he prayed that prayer for me. Not him.

Late this morning, I got to the hospital and found the exact opposite. Dad was sitting up in bed, color in his cheeks, the window blinds open with sun pouring into the room. One look at him and I knew God had done something.

The most obvious change? He's talkative. He's interested in us—in Mom. It's like he's been away for a long time. Now he's home. And more than anything, he wants to spend time with us. Can you believe it?

Best gift ever.

Friday morning—August 16

Our family is in celebration mode.

Two days ago Dad asked if he could spend time with each of us alone. Including our spouses and children. He also had a list—a small list—of people he wants to see from his shop. We're doing it, but taking it slow so it doesn't exhaust him.

The doctors and nurses have all seen the change in Dad.

Yesterday, his cardiologist said there's no reason to keep him in the hospital. "His heart function hasn't changed. It's still very weak." He suggested Dad go to rehab for a couple of weeks to be monitored. Dad told him he'd rather go home. As of now, that should happen sometime on Monday.

Biggest surprise?

He's spending a lot of time with Ellie and Mom. He's got them reading the Bible to him! His suggestion—not theirs. What can I say? We're all pretty stunned.

Saturday night—August 17

A lot has happened in a short time. Dad had a long talk with Mom the other day and they decided to change their wills. Somehow, they got their lawyer to comply. He came to the hospital late yesterday afternoon with a notary.

Also, Dad asked Ellie to call their Catholic priest. He's supposed to visit Dad sometime after church tomorrow.

Some of Dad's friends have come by. Others we asked to wait till next week when he's home and more rested. Dad was pretty insistent that family has to come first. By late today, I think he's talked to each of us.

But no one shocked us more than Mom.

From what Ellie and I could gather, Dad apologized to her. She tried to brush it aside, but Dad wouldn't let her. They talked a long time, making Mom cry—good tears, she said. But sad tears, deeply sad, for all the years they've missed.

Of all nights, tonight was the best.

There must've been fifteen of us packed in his room. I'm surprised they didn't kick us out. Dad was in rare form. We've all known Zane was his favorite. But not tonight—we were all his favorite. It's like we're living in a dream. The Lord has done what we never thought possible. All I can do is praise Him tonight. And ask— would You give us more time with him?

Sunday afternoon—August 18

Down day. He's tired.

He asked Mom to stay when Father Carey stopped by around 1:30. She said Dad asked for two things. Could he make his confession? And was it possible to commit his life to Christ this late in life? Father Carey assured him it was. He then spoke for a while on the tender mercies of God.

Afterward, rather than the customary giving of last rites, the priest anointed him with oil and prayed for his heart to be fully healed in Jesus' name. That's my prayer too.

Got to see Dad for a few minutes. Didn't stay long. He said he was tired and needed sleep. Told him I'd stop by later this evening.

Late Sunday night—August 18

Carol and I got to the hospital around seven. Mom, Ellie, and Ellie's husband, Tom, were there. Dad still looks tired, but the glimmer in his eyes hasn't left him. He's excited about going home tomorrow. "Can't come soon enough," he said.

Before we left, Dad asked if we could pray together. We held hands around his bed and—surprise again. This time, Dad prayed a simple prayer of blessing over us and our families. When he was done, he looked straight at Mom and said what I've never heard him say before.

"I love you, sweetheart."

Mom fell into his arms and sobbed.

I'll leave work by noon tomorrow so I can help bring Dad home. My heart is full tonight. The Lord has been so kind to us.

Walt sent a text message in the early hours of Monday morning: **Call me.** I did soon after I awoke. Walt said he'd heard from his mom.

"The moment the phone rang, I knew," he told me. "All she said was, 'He's home, Walt, he's home. Quietly, while he was sleeping, Jesus took him home.'"

QUESTIONS FOR REFLECTION

What do you think of Jesus' question? Why is it important for us to see the physical acts of mercy in order to receive the eternal mercy that makes us right with God?

Walt wanted the Lord to heal his dad's physical heart. Instead, he got to see the surprising transformation in his dad's spiritual and emotional heart. How has this happened in your life? Have you seen His mercy transform you? Others?

49

SURPRISING GENEROSITY

—⁓—

Reflections on Mark 2:12 and Luke 5:26

*And amazement seized them all, and they glorified
God and were filled with awe, saying,
"We have seen extraordinary things today."*

—LUKE 5:26 ESV

It's how the Bible begins. All God did was speak.

*Now, in a house in Capernaum, Jesus—the "Word made
flesh," "through whom all things were made" (see John 1:14, 3)—
did the same thing. He spoke to the paralytic. First, to heal his
soul. Second, to heal his body.*

*What was that like? What did the paralyzed man feel when
forgiveness entered his soul? And what happened to him when
the power of God rushed into his legs? Was it visible? Did he see
muscle suddenly appear, his legs swell with strength? Or was
there no external change at all, but now he could feel them? He
could move them. Maybe for the first time ever. And with it came
this impulse to get up on his feet and stand. Did he even know
how to do it—on his own, with no one helping him?*

And then it happened. There he was—standing!

*Were there gasps? Is that what "amazement" and "awe"
sound like at first? Did everyone in the house get up on their feet
too? Did they burst into applause? Were there shrieks of joy and
shouts of praise as they began "glorifying God" with all their heart?*

Did the same thing happen on the roof?

Did his four friends shout for joy as they saw him healed? Could they even contain themselves? Did they dance? Did they lift their voice and announce the news to everybody outside watching? What did they say? How did they say it?

Did the song of praise inside the house become the song of praise outside? It must have been infectious, for it is said that everyone began "glorifying God."

Everyone—it "seized them all."

And I wonder, does that mean the scribes and Pharisees too? Did they suddenly burst into praise with everybody else? This is what the prophets said would happen when Messiah came. The lame will "leap like a deer" and joy—"everlasting joy"—would come upon them (Isa. 35:6, 10). This joy, did it seize them?

This joy—did it change them?

The gospel accounts all seem to say no. The scribes and Pharisees would continue to oppose Jesus to the end. But does that mean all of them? Is it possible that sitting in the house that day were men like Joseph of Arimathea or Nicodemus—men who belonged to them but weren't like them?

Is it possible they too heard Jesus speak and the same thing happened? Just like the paralytic. They felt the power of Jesus Christ come into their souls. In the surprising generosity of God, they too were healed. And this joy—it did change them.

Changed them now. Changed them forever.

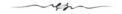

The funeral mass for Edmund Walter Pittman was held at St. Catherine of Sienna. The church was nearly full on a Thursday morning in late August.

Father Carey presided.

The service began quietly as the casket was carried by Ed's oldest friends to the front of the church. The priest walked behind, reading passages of hope and comfort from the Bible. After that, the music started. The sound of singing was robust and loud, feeling more like an Easter service than a mass for the dead.

More Scripture was read, this time by Ellie and Tom.

Father Carey then went to the pulpit. I did my best to record his words. After praying and welcoming family and friends, he started right in:

Well, look at this, will you? Ed Pittman finally came to church! 'Course, some of you may be saying, "'Bout the only way you'd get him here."

I couldn't agree more. After fifty-plus years as a member of this church, he said he could count the number of times he'd been here on two hands.

So I didn't expect much when Ellie called last week and said she wanted me to visit her father in the hospital. Generally, in my experience, in situations like this, the priest is there to comfort the family more than the dying. So, I went fully expecting the family wanted me there to administer last rites.

But I never did.

It wasn't Ellie who wanted me there. It was Ed. Now some of you are going to have a hard time believing that. You know Ed. Some of you have known him since he married and started a shop here in town fifty-six years ago. You know he wanted nothing to do with

God. He spent his Sundays on the golf course or in card games. He made fun of those who needed to lean on the "crutch of religion."

Those are his words, not mine.

Now listen carefully. Ed Pittman wanted to ask me if it was possible to give his life to Jesus Christ on his death bed. Did you hear that? That was his question to me. He said he'd already prayed with his son, Walt, to become a Christian and, after that prayer, something happened that surprised him. It may surprise you.

Ed Pittman told me he believed in God.

At once, I assured him that God "being rich in mercy, because of His great love with which He has loved us, even when we were dead in our transgressions, made us alive together with Christ (by grace you have been saved)" (Eph. 2:4–5). So, yes, I said. If the Lord extends mercy at our last hour, then the answer is yes.

"But this late in life?" he asked. "Is it really possible?"

My friends, it is possible. I rarely see it. Not like this. I stand here this morning to tell you that Ed Pittman was a changed man. God had mercy on him. Christ came into that crusty old heart of his and made him a new man. I saw it with my own eyes. I don't have any other words for it—it was miraculous.

And Ed knew it. I want you to know it.

Father Carey then pointed to Walt and asked him to join him at the pulpit. Walt came up, nervously cleared his throat, and began:

I came to faith in Jesus Christ in my early twenties. Soon after, my wife, Carol, taught me to love my father as Christ loved me. She said if Jesus could do that for me, I could do that for my dad. I didn't want to.

Dad wanted nothing to do with me growing up. So I decided, after high school, I wanted nothing to do with him either.

But Christ made a difference in my life. He wanted me to choose a different path. And so, I've spent a lifetime loving my dad by doing simple things. Like helping him around the house or taking care of Mom or doing whatever he needed.

But deep down, I wanted to do more for Dad. I tried telling him about Christ when our son Zane was sick in the hospital. But he wanted nothing to do with it. He said, and I'll never forget it, "That's not for me, Son." It broke my heart. I know God's mercy is more than taking care of our earthly needs. It's meant to bring us to God and open a door to heaven. And I wanted Dad in heaven.

So this past week in the hospital, I tried to tell him about Jesus again. And I don't know why it was different this time, but it was and I knew it. He knew it.

All I can tell you is that mercy came.

Walt's voice broke. He tried to gather himself but couldn't. Surprisingly, one of Ed's old friends stood up in the front row and went to Walt. He put his arm around him and turned to speak to the congregation:

A week ago, I'd have told you what we're hearing this morning is complete rubbish. It's not Ed. It's not the man we've known all these years. But last Friday, I got to see him in the hospital. And what these two men are saying—I got to see for myself. I don't understand it. I don't know what to make of it. And I've never said this in my entire life. But, praise the Lord, everybody. Praise the Lord!

And suddenly, we were all on our feet. All of us. Father Carey moved toward the casket and, with a beautiful baritone voice, began singing John Newton's old hymn, "Amazing Grace." We all did. People sang. People cried. And for a brief moment—whether it changed anybody or not—everlasting joy came.

Filling the church. Filling us all.

QUESTIONS FOR REFLECTION

How can we witness the Lord's power, be filled with amazement and awe, and not be forever changed by it? There are many stories like this in the Bible. Is this our story? If so, why does it happen?

Reflect on Ephesians 2:4–5. How has the God of mercy come to change you? Do you know something about worship—praising and glorifying God—as a result?

50

'TIS MERCY ALL

~~~

Reflections on Luke 5:25

*Immediately he got up before them, and picked up what
he had been lying on, and went home glorifying God.*

—LUKE 5:25

Jesus told him, "Arise. Take your mat. Walk. Go home."
And he did, quickly.

I wonder if he leapt into the air like a deer (see Isa. 35:6). I
wonder if his mouth filled with song and praise? I wonder if he,
like so many who were healed by Jesus, resisted the urge to fall
at His feet and worship Him?

But, no doubt, he did what he was told. He grabbed his mat.

Why did Jesus even mention the mat? He didn't have to. Or
possibly, He could've told the man to leave it right where it was
and never touch it again. But instead, He ordered the man to take
it into his hands and carry it home with him.

A sign and symbol of all he once was.

We don't even know his name. He's called "the paralytic" five
times in Mark's gospel. He's the man on the mat. It defines him.
He is, and always has been, branded by his disability. The mat
had been his life. It had been his everything.

And now, here it was, in his hands. He wasn't on it—he was
holding it! There weren't four friends, one on each corner. Or even

two at both ends. No, look! He was holding it, and he could hold it high—while standing!—showing everybody his days as a paralytic were over and a new life had begun by the power, mercy, and compassion of Jesus Christ.

Out he went. Out the front door. All by himself.

Did his four friends race off the roof to greet him as he came out? Did they embrace him? Did the crowd cheer? Did his friends go with him as he made his way through the masses of people outside? Did they follow him home shouting the praise of almighty God at the top of their lungs?

And the man—what was it like for him to run the streets of town, his legs strong, the wind in his face, and the rush of joy filling his heart? All because he couldn't wait for everybody on the street where he lived to see what the Lord had done for him.

He was an ambassador now. A missionary.

Sent by the Lord Jesus Christ to "go home to your people and report to them what great things the Lord has done for you, and how He had mercy on you" (Mark 5:19).

Now he could do what his four friends did for him. He could show mercy to them as he'd been shown mercy. Acts of kindness! Never failing love! Not once in a while – but always. He could now be friends with those who needed friends.

And more. He could be on the team that grabs the mat of others just like him. He can run the streets of town. He can climb on roofs and break right through them. He can do what his friends did for him.

He can bring them to Jesus!

And let mercy come again.

Time passes way too quickly. A few months after the funeral, Erilynne and I moved to pastor another church in a different state. Walt and I stayed in touch for a while, then not so much.

Hard to believe ten years have gone by.

A few days ago, I got home from work and found a handwritten letter from him. I opened it and saw a newspaper clipping of his mom's obituary with a photo taken years ago. Before reading it, I turned to his letter.

Dear Thad and Erilynne,

I hope you are well, my dear friends.

Carol and I wanted you to see this. Mom died peacefully about a week ago in the same hospital where Dad died. Her last years were good years.

Soon after you left, Mom moved in with us. All I can say is she surprised us. She never took off her wedding band. When she talked about Dad, she pictured him as the man she first loved and married. The same man she got to see the last week of his life. The years in between, she somehow quietly chose to forget.

I've tried to make sense of it. The best I can do is say: In Dad's crippling, we were all crippled. In his healing, we, too, were healed. I know it's true of me.

I have confidence now. I'm the same old Walt. I've never lost my passion for seniors. Micah 6:8 is still my favorite Bible verse. I choose "to love mercy."

Every day.

I'm convinced the Lord requires us to meet the needs of those around us. No matter who they are, or what they've done, or whether they respond to us or not. We never stop. We never forget the practical, hands-on care for all who suffer in this life—especially those who are poor, weak, lonely, sick, and afraid.

But, I'm telling you, Dad's story changed me.

There's a joy inside—an uncontainable joy. I want to see people come to faith in Christ just like Dad. I want the mercy that comes from heaven to touch their souls, too. So, at the nursing homes, it just came out of me. I'd find myself telling people my dad's story and how he came to faith in Jesus the last week of his life. "And if it could happen for a man like that," I'd say, "it can happen for you!" I took risks I never dreamed.

Risks that God honored. I got to see His mercy come again and again. Just like with Dad. I got to start Bible studies at the nursing homes. Pastors asked me to come to their churches and teach Christians the basic principles of how to bring people to faith in Jesus. And every time I do, that old hymn wells up in my soul:

> *'Tis mercy all, immense and free;*
> *For, O my God, it found out me.*
> *Amazing love, how can it be*
> *That Thou, my God, should die for me![1]*

I can't stop singing it! We're seeing more and more Christians choosing "to love mercy." Churches are rising up like a mighty army with all kinds of innovative ways to care for the practical needs of our community. And

*with it has come a new confidence to share the love of
Jesus Christ with people.*

*Stories! We're hearing stories everywhere of people
giving their lives to Christ. Every time, it reminds me
of Dad and fills my heart with thanksgiving and song.*

'Tis mercy all!

*And in that mercy, Carol and I send you both our love,
Walt*

As a postscript, he gave a phone number and said, "Call
me sometime?"

Erilynne and I decided to call after dinner. Before we
did, we went online and found Walt. Articles, pictures, and
a few social media pages. We clicked here, clicked there,
and one picture in particular caught my eye.

I could still see it. That frown deeply sculpted in his face.

"A gift from my father," he used to say.

"So your dad has it too?" I asked.

"No," he said. "It's mine. Years of heartache with him,
that's all."

It's how I remember Walt. For me, that frown was the
picture of the pain he bore because of his dad. And now, I
could see, time had not been kind to him. That frown had
deepened into an almost angry scowl.

Thankfully, they were home to answer our call.

One sound of his voice and we could hear the difference. There was joy in him like we'd never heard before.
The sound—almost what I imagine the man on the mat

sounded like when he tore out of the house and onto the streets.

Once crippled—then crippled no more.

And like him, Walt was a man on a mission—free, healed, and wanting nothing more than to run the streets telling everybody what Jesus had done for him.

"So, Walt, I have a question," I said that night.

"Ask away," he replied.

"I'm looking at your picture on the Internet. Why'd you decide to keep that frown on your face?"

He laughed and said, "Because I need it. All by itself, it tells the story of Dad and me and what our life was like together before mercy came. Before mercy surprised us both." And with that, he started singing loud, singing full:

> "'Tis mercy all, immense and free;
> For, O my God, it found out me."

QUESTIONS FOR REFLECTION

What is your "mat"? What is the sign and symbol of all you once were? Have you been or are you now known by your disability? Why did Jesus want the paralytic to embrace the mat? Is that He wants from us?

Will you choose today to love mercy? Will you let His mercy fill your heart until all you can do in life is show others the mercy He has shown you?

NOTE

1. Charles Wesley, "And Can It Be," 1738, public domain.

Where Bible and Life Meet

Thaddeus Barnum leads his readers through sixty engaging devotional reflections into the soul's most personal crossroads—where the Bible intersects life. In each reading crafted around 1 John, Barnum artfully connects the truth of biblical teaching, revealing and modeling the way of an authentic disciple.

In *Real Love*, Barnum guides us through understanding that God is love. For those tired of superficial love for God and neighbors, this transparently crafted book shines the light of Scripture upon a well-worn path for all disciples who would know and live real love.

Real Love

978-0-89827-914-6

978-0-89827-915-3 (e-book)

www.wphresources.com/reallove